LULU IN HOLLYWOOD

Lulu
IN HOLLYWOOD

EXPANDED EDITION

Louise Brooks

INTRODUCTION BY KENNETH TYNAN

University of Minnesota Press
Minneapolis

The University of Minnesota Press gratefully acknowledges the assistance of Thomas Gladysz, director of the Louise Brooks Society, in the publication of this book. The society's website can be found at www.pandorasbox.com.

First University of Minnesota Press edition, 2000

Published by the University of Minnesota Press
111 Third Avenue South, Suite 290
Minneapolis, MN 55401-2520
http://www.upress.umn.edu

A Cataloging-in-Publication record for this book is available from the Library of Congress.

Printed in the United States of America on acid-free paper

The University of Minnesota is an equal-opportunity educator and employer.

25 24 23 22 21   10 9

Contents

Introduction

The Girl in the Black Helmet

KENNETH TYNAN

NONE OF THIS WOULD HAVE HAPPENED if I had not noticed, while lying late in bed on a hot Sunday morning last year in Santa Monica and flipping through the TV guide for the impending week, that one of the local public-broadcasting channels had decided to show, at 1 P.M. that very January day, a film on which my fantasies had fed ever since I first saw it, a quarter of a century before. Even for Channel 28, it was an eccentric piece of programming. I wondered how many of my Southern Californian neighbors would be tempted to forgo their poolside champagne brunches, their bicycle jaunts along Ocean Front Walk, their health-food picnics in Topanga Canyon, or their surfboard battles with the breakers of Malibu in order to watch a silent picture, shot in Berlin just fifty years earlier, about an artless young hedonist who, meaning no harm, rewards her lovers—and eventually herself—with the prize of violent death. Although the film is a tragedy, it is also a celebration of the pleasure principle. Outside in the midday sunshine, California was celebrating the same principle, with the shadows of mortality left out.

I got to my set in time to catch the credits. The director: Georg Wilhelm Pabst, reigning maestro of German cinema in the late nineteen-twenties. The script: Adapted by Ladislaus Vajda from *Erdgeist (Earth Spirit)* and *Die Büchse der Pandora (Pandora's Box)*, two scabrously erotic plays written in the eighteen-nineties by Frank Wedekind. For his movie, Pabst chose the title of the later work, though the screenplay differed markedly from Wedekind's original text: *Pandora's Box* belongs among the few films that have succeeded in improving on theatrical chefs-d'œuvre. For his heroine, Lulu (the dominant figure in both plays), Pabst outraged a whole generation of German actresses by choosing a twenty-one-year-old girl from Kansas whom he had never met, who was currently working for Paramount in Hollywood, and who spoke not a word of any language other than English. This was Louise Brooks. She made only twenty-four films, in a movie career that began in 1925 and ended, with enigmatic suddenness, in 1938. Two of them were masterpieces: *Pandora's Box* and its immediate successor, also directed by Pabst—*The Diary of a Lost Girl*. Most, however, were assembly-line studio products. Yet around her, with a luxuriance that proliferates every year, a literature has grown up. I append a few excerpts:

> An actress who needed no directing, but could move across the screen causing the work of art to be born by her mere presence.
> —*Lotte H. Eisner, French critic*

> Her youthful admirers see in her an actress of brilliance, a luminescent personality, and a beauty unparalleled in film history.
> —*Kevin Brownlow, British director and movie historian*

> One of the most mysterious and potent figures in the history of the cinema . . . she was one of the first performers to penetrate to the heart of screen acting.
> —*David Thomson, British critic*

> Louise Brooks is the only woman who had the ability to transfigure no matter what film into a masterpiece. . . . Louise is the perfect apparition, the dream woman, the being without whom the cinema would be a poor thing. She is much more than a myth, she is a magical presence, a real phantom, the magnetism of the cinema.
> —*Ado Kyroit, French critic*

> Those who have seen her can never forget her. She is the modern actress par excellence. . . . As soon as she takes the screen, fiction disappears along with art, and one has the impression of being present at a documentary. The camera seems to have caught her by surprise, without her knowledge. She is the intelligence of the cinematic process, the perfect incarnation of that which is photogenic; she embodies all that the cinema rediscovered in its last years of silence: complete naturalness and complete simplicity. Her art is so pure that it becomes invisible.
> —*Henri Langlois, director of the Cinémathèque Française*

On Channel 28, I stayed with the film to its end, which is also Lulu's. Of the climactic sequence, so decorously understated, Louise Brooks once wrote, in *Sight & Sound*, "It is Christmas Eve and she is about to receive the gift which has been her dream since childhood. Death by a sexual maniac." When it was over, I switched channels and returned to the real world of game shows and pet-food commercials, relieved to find that the spell she cast was still as powerful as ever. Brooks reminds me of the scene in *Citizen Kane* where Everett Sloane, as Kane's aging business manager, recalls a girl in a white dress whom he saw in his youth when he was crossing over to Jersey on a ferry. They never met or spoke. "I only saw her for one second," he says, "and she didn't see me at all—but I'll bet a month hasn't gone by since that I haven't thought of that girl."

I had now, by courtesy of Channel 28, seen *Pandora's Box* for the third time. My second encounter with the film had taken place several years earlier, in France. Consulting my journal, I found the latter experience recorded with the baroque extravagance that seems to overcome all those who pay tribute to Brooks. I unflinchingly quote:

Infatuation with L. Brooks reinforced by second viewing of "Pandora." She has run through my life like a magnetic thread—this shameless urchin tomboy, this unbroken, unbreakable porcelain filly. She is a prairie princess, equally at home in a waterfront bar and in the royal suite at Neuschwanstein; a creature of impulse, a creature of impulses, a temptress with no pretensions, capable of dissolving into a giggling fit at a peak of erotic ecstasy; amoral but totally selfless, with that sleek jet cloche of hair that rings such a peal of bells in my subconscious. In short, the only star actress I can imagine either being enslaved by or wanting to enslave; and a dark lady worthy of any poet's devotion:

For I have sworn thee fair, and thought thee bright,
Who art as black as hell, as dark as night.

Some basic information about Rochester, New York: With two hundred sixty-three thousand inhabitants, it is the sixth-largest city in the state, bestriding the Genesee River at its outlet into Lake Ontario. Here, in the eighteen-eighties, George Eastman completed the experiments that enabled him to manufacture the Kodak camera, which, in turn, enabled ordinary people to capture monochrome images, posed or spontaneous, of the world around them. He was in at the birth of movies, too. The flexible strips of film used in Thomas Edison's motion-picture machine were first produced by Eastman, in 1889. Rochester is plentifully dotted with monuments to the creator of the Kodak, among them a palatial

Georgian house, with fifty rooms and a lofty neoclassical portico, that he built for himself in 1905. When he died, in 1932, he left his mansion to the University of Rochester, of whose president it became the official home. Shortly after the Second World War, Eastman House took on a new identity. It opened its doors to the public and offered, to quote from its brochure, "the world's most important collection of pictures, films, and apparatus showing the development of the art and technology of photography." In 1972, it was imposingly renamed the International Museum of Photography. Its library now contains around five thousand movies, many of them unique copies, and seven of them—a larger number than any other archive can boast—featuring Louise Brooks. Hence I decide to pay a visit to the city, where I check in at a motel in the late spring of 1978. Thanks to the generous cooperation of Dr. John B. Kuyper, the director of the museum's film department, I am to see its hoard of Brooks pictures—six of them new to me—within the space of two days. Screenings will be held in the Dryden Theatre, a handsome auditorium that was added to the main building in 1950 as a gift from Eastman's niece, Ellen Andrus, and her husband, George Dryden.

On the eve of Day One, I mentally recap what I have learned of Brooks's early years. Born in 1906 in Cherryvale, Kansas, she was the second of four children sired by Leonard Brooks, a hardworking lawyer of kindly disposition and diminutive build, for whom she felt nothing approaching love. She herself was never more than five feet two and a half inches tall, but she raised her stature onscreen by wearing heels as high as six inches. Her mother, née Myra Rude, was the eldest of nine children, and she warned Mr. Brooks before their marriage that she had spent her entire life thus far looking after kid brothers and sisters, that she had no intention of repeating the experience with children of her own, and that any progeny she might bear him would, in effect, have to fend for themselves.

The result, because Myra Brooks was a woman of high spirits who took an infectious delight in the arts, was not a cold or neglectful upbringing. Insistent on liberty for herself, she passed on a love of liberty to her offspring. Louise absorbed it greedily. Pirouetting appealed to her; encouraged by her mother, she took dancing lessons, and by the age of ten she was making paid appearances at Kiwanis and Rotary festivities. At fifteen, already a beauty sui generis, as surviving photographs show, with her hair, close-cropped at the nape to expose what Christopher Isherwood has called "that unique imperious neck of hers," cascading in ebony bangs down the high, intelligent forehead, and descending on either side of her eyes in spit curls slicked forward at the cheekbones, like a pair of enameled parentheses—at fifteen, she left high school and went to New York with her dance teacher.

There she successfully auditioned for the Denishawn Dancers, which had been founded in 1915 by Ruth St. Denis and Ted Shawn, and was by far the most adventurous dance company in America. She started out as a student, but soon graduated to full membership in the troupe, with which she toured the country from 1922 to 1924. One of her fellow dancers, Martha Graham, became a life-long friend. "I learned to act while watching Martha Graham dance," she said later, in an interview with Kevin Brownlow, "and I learned to move in film from watching Chaplin."

Suddenly, however, the discipline involved in working for Denishawn grew oppressive. Brooks was fired for lacking a sense of vocation, and the summer of 1924 found her back in New York, dancing in the chorus of George White's *Scandals*. After three months of this, a whim seized her, and she embarked without warning for London, where she performed the Charleston at the Café de Paris, near Piccadilly Circus. By New York standards, she thought Britain's Bright Young Things a moribund bunch, and when Evelyn Waugh wrote *Vile Bodies* about them, she said that only a genius could have made a masterpiece out of such glum material.

Early in 1925, with no professional prospects, she sailed for Manhattan on borrowed money, only to be greeted by Florenz Ziegfeld with the offer of a job in a musical comedy called *Louie the 14th*, starring Leon Errol. She accepted, but the pattern of her subsequent behavior left no doubt that what she meant by liberty and independence was what others defined as irresponsibility and self-indulgence. Of the director of *Louie the 14th*, she afterward wrote, again for *Sight & Sound*: "He detested all of Ziegfeld's spoiled beauties, but most of all me because on occasion, when I had other commitments, I would wire my non-appearance to the theatre." In May 1925, she made her movie debut at the Paramount Astoria Studio on Long Island, playing a bit part in *The Street of Forgotten Men*, of which no print is known to exist. She has written a vivid account of filmmaking in its Long Island days:

The stages were freezing in the winter, steaming hot in the summer. The dressing rooms were windowless cubicles. We rode on the freight elevator, crushed by lights and electricians. But none of that mattered, because the writers, directors, and cast were free from all supervision. Jesse Lasky,

Adolph Zukor, and Walter Wanger never left the Paramount office on Fifth Avenue, and the head of production never came on the set. There were writers and directors from Princeton and Yale. Motion pictures did not consume us. When work finished, we dressed in evening clothes, dined at the Colony or "21," and went to the theatre.

The difference in Hollywood was that the studio was run by B. P. Schulberg, a coarse exploiter who propositioned every actress and policed every set. To love books was a big laugh. There was no theatre, no opera, no concerts—just those god-damned movies.

Despite Brooks's erratic conduct in *Louie the 14th,* Ziegfeld hired her to join Will Rogers and W. C. Fields in the 1925 edition of his *Follies.* It proved to be her last Broadway show. One of her many admirers that year was the atrabilious wit Herman Mankiewicz, then employed as second-string drama critic of the *Times.* Blithely playing truant from the *Follies,* she attended the opening of *No, No, Nanette* on Mankiewicz's arm. As the houselights faded, her escort, who was profoundly drunk, announced his intention of falling asleep and asked Brooks to make notes on the show for use in his review. She obliged, and the *Times* next day echoed her opinion that *No, No, Nanette* was "a highly meritorious paradigm of its kind." (Somewhat cryptically, the review added that the score contained "more familiar quotations from itself . . . than even *Hamlet.*")

Escapades like this did nothing to endear Brooks to the other, more dedicated Ziegfeld showgirls, but an abiding intimacy grew up between her and W. C. Fields, in whose dressing room she was always graciously received. Later, in a passage that tells us as much about its author as about her subject, she wrote:

He was an isolated person. As a young man he stretched out his hand to Beauty and Love and they thrust it away. Gradually he reduced reality to exclude all but his work, filling the gaps with alcohol whose dim eyes transformed the world into a distant view of harmless shadows. He was also a solitary person. Years of traveling alone around the world with his juggling act taught him the value of solitude and the release it gave his mind. . . . Most of his life will remain unknown. But the history of no life is a jest.

In September 1925, the *Follies* left town on a national tour. Brooks stayed behind and sauntered through the role of a bathing beauty in a Paramount movie called *The American Venus.* Paramount and M-G-M were both pressing her to sign five-year contracts, and she looked for advice to Walter Wanger, one of the former company's top executives, with whom she was having an intermittent affair. "If, at this crucial moment in my career," she said long afterward in *London Magazine*, "Walter had given me some faith in my screen personality and my acting ability, he might have saved me from further mauling by the beasts who prowled Broadway and Hollywood." Instead, he urged her to take the Metro offer, arguing that if she chose Paramount everyone would assume that she had got the job by sharing his bed and that her major attribute was not talent but sexual accessibility. Incensed by his line of reasoning, she defiantly signed with Paramount.

In the course of twelve months (during which Brooks's friend Humphrey Bogart, seven years her senior, was still laboring on Broadway, with four seasons to wait before the dawn of his film career), Brooks made six full-length pictures. The press began to pay court to her. *Photoplay,* whose reporter she received reclining in bed, said of her, "She is so very Manhattan. Very young. Exquisitely hard-boiled. Her black eyes and sleek black hair are as brilliant as Chinese lacquer. Her skin is white as a camellia. Her legs are lyric."

She worked with several of the bright young directors who gave Paramount its reputation for sophisticated comedy, e.g., Frank Tuttle, Malcolm St. Clair, and Edward Sutherland. Chronologically, the list of her credits ran as follows:

- *The American Venus,* for Tuttle, who taught her that the way to get laughs was to play perfectly straight; he directed Bebe Daniels in four movies and Clara Bow in six.
- *A Social Celebrity,* for St. Clair, who cast Brooks opposite the immaculately caddish Adolphe Menjou, of whose style she later remarked, "He never felt anything. He used to say, 'Now I do Lubitsch No. 1,' 'Now I do Lubitsch No. 2.' And that's exactly what he did. You felt nothing, working with him, and yet see him on the screen—he was a great actor."
- *It's the Old Army Game,* for Sutherland, who had been Chaplin's directorial assistant on *A Woman of Paris,* and who made five pictures with W. C. Fields, of which this was the first, and of which the third, *International House,* is regarded by many Fieldsian authorities as the Master's crowning achievement. Brooks married Sutherland, a hard-drinking playboy, in 1926—an error that was rectified inside two years by divorce.
- *The Show-Off,* for St. Clair, adapted from the Broadway hit by George Kelly.

- *Just Another Blonde*, on loan to First National.
- And, finally, to round off the year's work, *Love 'Em and Leave 'Em*, for Tuttle, the first Brooks film of which Eastman House has a copy. Here begin my notes on the sustained and solitary Brooks banquet that the museum laid before me.

Day One

Evelyn Brent is the nominal star of *Love 'Em and Leave 'Em,* a slick and graceful comedy about Manhattan shopgirls, but light-fingered Louise, as Brent's jazz-baby younger sister, steals the picture with bewitching insouciance. She is twenty, and her body is still plump, quite husky enough for work in the fields; but the face, framed in its black proscenium arch of hair, is already Lulu's in embryo, especially when she dons a white top hat to go to a costume ball (at which she dances a definitive Charleston). The plot calls for her to seduce her sister's boyfriend, a feckless window dresser, and she does so with that fusion of amorality and innocence which was to become her trademark. (During these scenes, I catch myself humming a tune from *Pins and Needles*: "I used to be on the daisy chain, now I'm a chain-store daisy.") Garbo could give us innocence, and Dietrich amorality, on the grandest possible scale; only Brooks could play the simple, unabashed hedonist, whose appetite for pleasure is so radiant that even when it causes suffering to her and others we cannot find it in ourselves to reproach her.

Most actresses tend to pass moral judgments on the characters they play. Their performances issue tacit commands to the audience: "Love me," "Hate me," "Laugh at me," "Weep with me," and so forth. We get none of this from Brooks, whose presence before the camera merely declares, "Here I am. Make what you will of me." She does not care what we think of her. Indeed, she ignores us. We seem to be spying on unrehearsed reality, glimpsing what the great photographer Henri Cartier-Bresson later called "le moment qui se sauve." In the best of her silent films, Brooks—with no conscious intention of doing so—is reinventing the art of screen acting.

I suspect that she was helped rather than hindered by the fact that she never took a formal acting lesson. "When I acted, I hadn't the slightest idea of what I was doing," she said once to Richard Leacock, the documentary filmmaker. "I was simply playing myself, which is the hardest thing in the world to do—if you *know* that it's hard. I didn't, so it seemed easy. I had nothing to unlearn. When I first worked with Pabst, he was furious, because he approached people intellectually and you couldn't approach me intellectually, because there was nothing to approach." To watch Brooks is to recall Oscar Wilde's Lady Bracknell, who observes, "Ignorance is like a delicate, exotic fruit; touch it and the bloom is gone."

Rereading the above paragraphs, I pause at the sentence "She does not care what we think of her." Query: Was it precisely this quality, which contributed so much to her success on the screen, that enabled her, in later years, to throw that success so lightly away?

To return to Frank Tuttle's film: Tempted by a seedy and lecherous old horse-player who lives in her rooming house, Brooks goes on a betting spree with funds raised by her fellow shopgirls in aid of the Women's Welfare League. The aging gambler is played by Osgood Perkins (father of Tony), of whom Brooks said to Kevin Brownlow years afterward, "The best actor I ever worked with was Osgood Perkins . . . You know what makes an actor great to work with? Timing. You don't have to feel anything. It's like dancing with a perfect dancing partner. Osgood Perkins would give you a line so that you would react perfectly. It was timing—because *emotion means nothing*" (emphasis mine). This comment reveals what Brooks has learned about acting in the cinema: emotion per se, however deeply felt, is not enough. It is what the actor shows—the contraband that he or she can smuggle past the camera—that matters to the audience. A variation of this dictum cropped up in the mouth of John Striebel's popular comic-strip heroine Dixie Dugan, who was based on Brooks and first appeared in 1926. Bent on getting a job in "The Zigfold Follies," Dixie reflected, "All there is to this Follies racket is to *be cool and look hot*." Incidentally, Brooks's comparison of Perkins with a dancing partner reminds me of a remark she once made about Fatty Arbuckle, who, under the assumed name of William Goodrich, apathetically directed her in a 1931 two-reeler called *Windy Riley Goes to Hollywood*: "He sat in his chair like a man dead. He had been very nice and sweetly dead ever since the scandal that ruined his career . . . Oh, I thought he was magnificent in films. He was a wonderful dancer—a wonderful ballroom dancer in his heyday. It was like floating in the arms of a huge doughnut."

What images do I retain of Brooks in *Love 'Em and Leave 'Em*? Many comedic details, e.g., the scene in which she fakes tears of contrition by furtively dabbling her cheeks with water from a handily placed goldfish bowl, and our last view of her, with all her sins unpunished, merrily sweeping off in a Rolls-Royce with the owner of the department store. And, throughout, every closeup of that blameless, unblemished face.

In 1927, Brooks moved with Paramount to Hollywood and played in four pictures: *Evening Clothes* (with Menjou), *Rolled Stockings, The City Gone Wild,* and *Now We're in the Air,* none of which is in the Eastman vaults. To commemorate that year, I have a publicity photo taken at a house Brooks rented in Laurel Canyon: poised on tiptoe with arms outstretched, she stands on the diving board of her pool, wearing a one-piece black bathing suit with a tight white belt, and looking like a combination of Odette and Odile in some modern-dress version of *Swan Lake.*

Early in 1928, she was lent to Fox for a picture (happily preserved by the museum) that was to change her career—*A Girl in Every Port,* written and directed by Howard Hawks, who had made his first film only two years before. Along with Carole Lombard, Rita Hayworth, Jane Russell, and Lauren Bacall, Brooks thus claims a place among the actresses on David Thomson's list (in his *Biographical Dictionary of Film*) of performers who were "either discovered or brought to new life by Hawks." As in *Love 'Em and Leave 'Em,* she plays an amoral pleasure-lover, but this time the mood is much darker. Her victim is Victor McLaglen, a seagoing roughneck engaged in perpetual sexual rivalry with his closest friend (Robert Armstrong); the embattled relationship between the two men brings to mind the skirmishing of Flagg and Quirt in *What Price Glory?,* which was filmed with McLaglen in 1926. In *A Girl in Every Port,* McLaglen, on a binge in Marseilles, sees a performance by an open-air circus whose star turn is billed as "Mam'selle Godiva, Neptune's Bride and the Sweetheart of the Sea." The submarine coquette is, of course, Brooks, looking svelter than of old, and clad in tights, spangled panties, tiara, and black velvet cloak. Her act consists of diving off the top of a ladder into a shallow tank of water. Instantly besotted, the bully McLaglen becomes the fawning lapdog of this "dame of class." He proudly introduces her to Armstrong, who, unwilling to wreck his buddy's illusions, refrains from revealing that the lady's true character, as he knows from a previous encounter with her, is that of a small-time gold-digger. In a scene charged with the subtlest eroticism, Brooks sits beside Armstrong on a sofa and coaxes McLaglen to clean her shoes. He readily obeys. As he does so, she begins, softly, reminiscently, but purposefully, to fondle Armstrong's thigh. To these caresses Armstrong does not respond, but neither does he reject them. With one man at her feet and another at her fingertips, she is like a cat idly licking its lips over two bowls of cream. This must surely have been the sequence that convinced Pabst, when the film was shown in Berlin, that he had found the actress he wanted for *Pandora's Box.* By the end of the picture, Brooks has turned the two friends into mortal enemies, reducing McLaglen to a state of murderous rage mixed with grief which Emil Jannings could hardly have bettered. There is no melodrama in her exercise of sexual power. No effort, either: she is simply following her nature.

After her fling with Fox, Paramount cast its young star (now aged twenty-one) in another downbeat triangle drama, *Beggars of Life,* to be directed by another young director, William Wellman. Like Hawks, he was thirty-two years old. (The cinema is unique among the arts in that there was a time in its history when almost all its practitioners were young. This was that time.) At first, the studio had trouble tracing Brooks's whereabouts. Having just divorced Edward Sutherland, she had fled to Washington with a new lover—George Marshall, a millionaire laundry magnate, who later became the owner of the Redskins football team. When she was found, she immediately returned to the Coast, though her zest for work was somewhat drained by a strong antipathy to one of her co-stars (Richard Arlen, with whom she had appeared in *Rolled Stockings*) and by overt hostility from Wellman, who regarded her as a dilettante. Despite these malign auguries, *Beggars of Life*—available at Eastman House—turned out to be one of her best films.

Adapted from a novel by Jim Tully, it foreshadows the Depression movies of the thirties. Brooks plays the adopted daughter of a penniless old farmer who attempts, one sunny morning, to rape her. Seizing a shotgun, she kills him. As she is about to escape, the crime is discovered by a tramp (Arlen) who knocks at the door in search of food. They run away together, with Brooks wearing oversized masculine clothes, topped off by a large peaked cap. (This was her first serious venture into the rich territory of sexual ambiguity, so prosperously cultivated in later years by Garbo, Dietrich, et al.) Soon they fall in with a gang of hoboes, whose leader—a ferocious but teachable thug, beautifully played by Wallace Beery—forms the third point of the triangle. He sees through Brooks's disguise and proposes that since the police already know about her male imposture, it would be safer to dress her as a girl. He goes in search of female attire, but what he brings back is marginally too young: a gingham dress and a bonnet tied under the chin, in which Brooks looks like a woman masquerading as a child, a sort of adult Lolita. She stares at us in her new gear, at once innocent and gravely perverse. The rivalry for her affection comes to its height when Beery pulls a gun and tells Arlen to hand her over. Brooks jumps between them, protecting Arlen, and explains that she would prefer death to life without him. We believe her; and so, to his own befuddled amazement, does Beery. There is really no need for the title in which he says that he has often heard about love but never until now known what it was. He puts his gun away and lets them go.

Footnote: During the transvestite scenes, several dangerous feats were performed for Brooks by a stunt man named Harvey. One night, attracted by his flamboyant courage, she slept with him. After breakfast next day, she strolled out onto the porch of the hotel in the California village where the location sequences were being shot. Harvey was there, accompanied by a group of hoboes in the cast. He rose and gripped her by the arm. "Just a minute, Miss Brooks," he said loudly. "I've got something to ask you. I guess you know my job depends on my health." He then named a Paramount executive whom Brooks had never met, and continued, "Everybody knows you're his girl and he has syphilis, and what I want to know is: Do you have syphilis?" After a long and frozen pause, he added, "Another reason I want to know is that my girl is coming up at noon to drive me back to Hollywood." Brooks somehow withdrew to her room without screaming. Events like these may account for the lack of agonized regret with which she prematurely ended her movie career. Several years later, after she had turned down the part that Jean Harlow eventually played in Wellman's *The Public Enemy,* she ran into the director in a New York bar. "You always hated making pictures, Louise," he said sagely. She did not bother to reply that it was not pictures she hated but Hollywood.

The Canary Murder Case (directed by Malcolm St. Clair from a script based on S. S. Van Dine's detective story, with William Powell as Philo Vance; not in the Eastman collection) was the third, and last, American movie that Brooks made in 1928. By now, her face was beginning to be internationally known, and the rushes of this film indicated that Paramount would soon have a major star on its hands. At the time, the studio was preparing to take the plunge into talkies. As Brooks afterward wrote in *Image* (a journal sponsored by Eastman House), front offices all over Hollywood saw in this radical change "a splendid opportunity . . . for breaking contracts, cutting salaries, and taming the stars." In the autumn of 1928, when her own contract called for a financial raise, B. P. Schulberg, the West Coast head of Paramount, summoned her to his office and said that the promised increase could not be granted in the new situation. *The Canary Murder Case* was being shot silent, but who knew whether Brooks could speak? (A fragile argument, since her voice was of bell-like clarity.) He presented her with a straight choice: either to continue at her present figure (seven hundred and fifty dollars a week) or to quit when the current picture was finished. To Schulberg's surprise, she chose to quit. Almost as an afterthought, he revealed when she was rising to leave that he had lately received from G. W. Pabst a bombardment of cabled requests for her services in *Pandora's Box,* all of which he had turned down.

Then forty-three years old, Pabst had shown an extraordinary flair for picking and molding actresses whose careers were upward bound; Asta Nielsen, Brigitte Helm, and Greta Garbo (in her third film, *The Joyless Street,* which was also her first outside Sweden) headed a remarkable list. Unknown to Schulberg, Brooks had already heard about the Pabst offer—and the weekly salary of a thousand dollars that went with it—from her lover, George Marshall, whose source was a gossipy director at M-G-M. She coolly told Schulberg to inform Pabst that she would soon be available. "At that very hour in Berlin," she wrote later in *Sight & Sound*, "Marlene Dietrich was waiting with Pabst in his office." This was two years before *The Blue Angel* made Dietrich a star. What she crucially lacked, Pabst felt, was the innocence he wanted for his Lulu. In his own words, "Dietrich was too old and too obvious—one sexy look and the picture would become a burlesque. But I gave her a deadline, and the contract was about to be signed when Paramount cabled saying I could have Louise Brooks." The day that shooting ended on *The Canary Murder Case,* Brooks raced out of Hollywood en route for Berlin, there to work for a man who was one of the four or five leading European directors but of whom a few weeks earlier she had never heard.

Pandora's Box, with which I had my fourth encounter at Eastman House, could easily have emerged as a cautionary tale about a *grande cocotte* whose reward is the wages of sin. That seems to have been the impression left by Wedekind's two Lulu plays, which were made into a film in 1922 (not by Pabst) with Asta Nielsen in the lead. Summing up her predecessor's performance, Brooks said, "She played in the eye-rolling style of European silent acting. Lulu the man-eater devoured her sex victims . . . and then dropped dead in an acute attack of indigestion." The character obsessed many artists of the period. In 1928, Alban Berg began work on his twelve-tone opera *Lulu,* the heart of which, beneath the stark and stylized sound patterns, was blatantly theatrical, throbbing with romantic agony. Where the Pabst–Brooks version of the Lulu story differs from the others is in its moral coolness. It assumes neither the existence of sin nor the necessity for retribution. It presents a series of events in which all the participants are seeking happiness, and it suggests that Lulu, whose notion of happiness is momentary fulfillment through sex, is not less admirable than those whose quest is for wealth or social advancement.

First sequence: Lulu in the Art Deco apartment in Berlin where she is kept by Peter Schön, a middle-aged newspaper proprietor. (In this role, the great Fritz Kortner, bulky but urbane, effortless in the exercise of power over everyone but his mistress, gives one of the cinema's most accurate and objective portraits of a capitalist potentate.) Dressed in a peignoir, Lulu is casually flirting with a man who has come to read the gas meter when the doorbell rings and Schigolch enters—a squat and shabby old man who was once Lulu's lover but is now down on his luck. She greets him with delight; as the disgruntled gas man departs, she swoops to rest on Schigolch's lap with the grace of a swan. The protective curve of her neck is unforgettable. Producing a mouth organ, Schigolch strikes up a tune, to which she performs a brief, Dionysiac, and authentically improvised little dance. (Until this scene was rehearsed, Pabst had no idea that Brooks was a trained dancer.) Watching her, I recollect something that Schigolch says in Wedekind's original text, though not in the film: "The animal is the only genuine thing in man. . . . What you have experienced as an animal, no misfortune can ever wrest from you. It remains yours for life." From the window, he points out a burly young man on the sidewalk: this is a friend of his named Rodrigo, a professional athlete who would like to work with her in an adagio act.

Unheralded, Peter Schön lets himself into the apartment, and Lulu has just time to hide Schigolch on the balcony with a bottle of brandy. Schön has come to end his affair with Lulu, having decided to make a socially advantageous match with the daughter of a Cabinet minister. In Lulu's reaction to the news there is no fury. She simply sits on a sofa and extends her arms toward him with something like reassurance. Unmoved at first, Schön eventually responds, and they begin to make love. The drunken Schigolch inadvertently rouses Lulu's pet dog to a barking fit, and this disturbance provokes the hasty exit of Schön. On the stairs, he passes the muscle man Rodrigo, whom Schigolch presents to Lulu. Rodrigo flexes his impressive biceps, on which she gleefully swings, like a schoolgirl gymnast.

A scene in Schön's mansion shows us his son Alwa (Francis Lederer, in his pre-Hollywood days) busily composing songs for his new musical revue. Alwa is joined by the Countess Geschwitz (Alice Roberts), a tight-lipped lesbian who is designing the costumes. Lulu dashes in to announce her plans for a double act with Rodrigo, and it is immediately clear that both Alwa and the Countess have eyes for her. She strolls on into Peter Schön's study, where she picks up from the desk a photograph of his bride-to-be. Typically, she studies it with genuine interest; there's no narrowing of eyes or curling of lip. Peter Schön, who has entered the room behind her, snatches the picture from her hands and orders her to leave. Before doing so, she mischievously invents a rendezvous next day with Alwa, whom she kisses, full on the mouth, to the young man's embarrassed bewilderment. With a toss of the patent-leather hair and a glance, half-playful, half-purposeful, at Alwa, she departs. Alwa asks his father why he doesn't marry her. Rather too explosively to carry conviction, Peter replies that one doesn't marry women like that. He proposes that Alwa give her a featured role in the revue, and guarantees that his newspapers will make her a star. Alwa is overjoyed; but when his father warns him at all costs to beware of her, he quits the room in tongue-tied confusion.

So much for the exposition; the principal characters and the main thrust of the action have been lucidly established. Note that Lulu, for all her seductiveness, is essentially an exploited creature, not an exploiter; also that we are not (nor shall we ever be) invited to feel sorry for her. I've already referred to her birdlike movements and animal nature; let me add that in the context of the plot as a whole she resembles a glittering tropical fish in a tank full of predators. For the remainder of this synopsis, I'll confine myself to the four great set pieces on which the film's reputation rests.

1. Intermission at the opening night of Alwa's revue. Pabst catches the backstage panic of scene-shifting and costume-changing with a kaleidoscopic brilliance that looks forward to Orson Welles's handling, twelve years later, of the operatic debut of Susan Alexander Kane. Alwa and Geschwitz are there, reveling in what is obviously going to be a hit. Peter Schön escorts Marie, his fiancée, through the pass door to share the frenzy. Lulu, changing in the wings, catches sight of him and smiles. Stricken with embarrassment, he cuts her and leads Marie away. This treatment maddens Lulu, and she refuses to go on with the show: "I'll dance for the whole world, but not in front of that woman." She takes refuge in the property room, whither Peter follows her. Leaning against the wall, she sobs, shaking her head mechanically from side to side, and then flings herself onto a pile of cushions, which she kicks and pummels. Despite her tantrum, she is watching Schön's every move. When he lights a cigarette to calm himself, she snaps, "Smoking's not allowed in here," and gives him a painful hack on the ankle. The mood of the scene swings from high histrionics through sly comedy to voluptuous intimacy. Soon Schön and Lulu are laughing, caressing, wholeheartedly making love. At this point, the door opens, framing Marie and Alwa. Unperturbed, Lulu rises in triumph, gathers up her costume, and sweeps past them to go onstage. Peter Schön's engagement is obviously over.

2. The wedding reception. Lulu is in a snow-white bridal gown, suggesting less a victorious *cocotte* than a girl celebrating her First Communion. Peter's wealthy friends flock admiringly round her. She dances cheek to cheek with Geschwitz, who rabidly adores her. (The Belgian actress Alice Roberts, here playing what may be the first explicit lesbian in movie history, refused point-blank to look at Brooks with the requisite degree of lust. To solve the problem, Pabst stood in her line of vision, told her to regard him with passionate intensity, and photographed her in closeups, which he then intercut with shots of Brooks. Scenes like these presented no difficulty to Brooks herself. She used to say of a young woman I'll call Fritzi LaVerne, one of her best friends in the *Follies,* "She liked boys when she was sober and girls when she was drunk. I never heard a man or a woman pan her in bed, so she must have been very good." A shocked Catholic priest once asked Brooks how she felt playing a sinner like Lulu. "Feel!" she said gaily. "I felt fine! It all seemed perfectly normal to me." She explained to him that although she herself was not a lesbian, she had many chums of that persuasion in Ziegfeld's chorus line, and added, "I knew two millionaire publishers, much like Schön in the film, who backed shows to keep themselves well supplied with Lulus.")

The action moves to Peter's bedroom, where Schigolch and Rodrigo are drunkenly scattering roses over the nuptial coverlet. Lulu joins them, and something between a romp and an orgy seems imminent. It is halted by the entrance of the bridegroom. Appalled, he gropes for a gun in a nearby desk and chases the two men out of his house. The other guests, shocked and aghast, rapidly depart. When Peter returns to the bedroom, he finds Alwa with his head in Lulu's lap, urging her to run away with him. The elder Schön orders his son to leave. As soon as Alwa has left, there follows, between Kortner and Brooks, a classic demonstration of screen acting as the art of visual ellipsis. With the minimum of overt violence, a struggle for power is fought out to the death. Schön advances on Lulu, presses the gun into her hand, and begs her to commit suicide. As he grips her fingers in his, swearing to shoot her like a dog if she lacks the courage to do it herself, she seems almost hypnotized by the desperation of his grief. You would think them locked in an embrace until Lulu suddenly stiffens, a puff of smoke rises between them, and Schön slumps to the floor. Alwa bursts in and rushes to his father, from whose lips a fat thread of blood slowly trickles. The father warns Alwa that he will be the next victim. Gun in hand, Lulu stares at the body, wide-eyed and transfixed. Brooks wrote afterward that Pabst always used concrete phrases to get the emotional responses he wanted. In this case, the key image he gave her was "das Blut." "Not the murder of my husband," she wrote, "but the sight of the blood determined the expression on my face." What we see is not *Vénus toute entière à sa proie attachée* but a petrified child.

3. Trial and flight. Lulu is sentenced to five years' imprisonment for manslaughter, but as the judge pronounces the sentence, her friends, led by Geschwitz, set off a fire alarm, and in the ensuing courtroom chaos she escapes. With perfect fidelity to her own willful character, Lulu, in defiance of movie cliché, comes straight back to Schön's house, where she acts like a debutante relaxing after a ball—lighting a cigarette, idly thumbing through a fashion magazine, trying out a few dance steps, opening a wardrobe and stroking a new fur coat, running a bath and immersing herself in it. Only Brooks, perhaps, could have carried off this solo sequence—so unlike the behavior expected of criminals on the run—with such ingrained conviction and such lyrical aplomb. Now Alwa arrives and is astounded to find her at the scene of the crime. The two decide to flee together to Paris. No sooner have they caught the train, however, than they are recognized by a titled pimp, who blackmails them into accompanying him aboard a gambling ship. Geschwitz, Schigolch, and the tediously beefy Rodrigo are also afloat, and for a while the film lurches into melodrama—sub-Dostoevski with a touch of ship's Chandler. Rodrigo threatens to expose Lulu unless she sleeps with him; the Countess, gritting her teeth, distracts his attention by making love to him herself—an unlikely coupling—after which she disdainfully kills him. Meanwhile, the pimp is arranging to sell Lulu to an Egyptian brothel-keeper. Anxious to save her from this fate, Alwa frenetically cheats at cards and is caught with a sleeve full of aces. The police arrive just too late to prevent Alwa, Lulu, and Schigolch from escaping in a rowboat. For the shipboard episode, Pabst cajoled Brooks, much against her will, into changing her coiffure. The spit curls disappeared; the black bangs were parted, waved, and combed back to expose her forehead. These cardinal errors of taste defaced the icon. It was as if an Italian master had painted the Virgin and left out the halo.

4. London and catastrophe. The East End, icy and fogbound, on Christmas Eve. The Salvation Army is out in force, playing carols and distributing food to the poor. A sallow, mournfully handsome young man moves aimlessly through the crowds. He gives cash for the needy to an attractive Army girl, and gets in return a candle and a sprig of mistletoe. Posters on the walls warn the women of London against going out unescorted at night: there is a mass murderer at large. In a garret close by, its broken skylight covered by a flapping rag, Lulu lives in squalor with Alwa and Schigolch. The room is unfurnished except for a camp bed, an armchair, and a kitchen table with an oil lamp, a few pieces of chipped crockery, and a bread knife. Lulu's curls and bangs have been restored, but her clothes are threadbare: all three exiles are on the verge of starvation. Reduced by now to prostitution, Lulu ventures down into the street, where she accosts the young wanderer we have already met. He follows her up the stairs but stops halfway, as if reluctant to go farther. We see that he is holding behind his back a switchblade knife, open. Lulu proffers her hand and leans encouragingly toward him. Her smile is lambent and beckoning. Hesitantly, he explains that he has no money. With transparent candor, she replies that it doesn't matter: she likes him. Unseen by Lulu, he releases his grip on the knife and lets it fall into the stairwell. She leads him into the attic, which Alwa and Schigolch have tactfully vacated.

The scene that follows is tender, even buoyant, but unsoftened by sentimentality. The cold climax, when it comes, is necessary and inevitable. Ripper and victim relax like familiar lovers. He leans back in the armchair and stretches out his hand; she leaps onto his lap, landing with both knees bent, as weightless as a chamois. Her beauty has never looked more ripe. While they happily flirt, he allows her to pry into his pockets, from which she extracts the gifts he received from the Salvation Army. She lights the candle and places it ceremonially on the table, with the mistletoe beside it. In a deep and peaceful embrace, they survey the tableau. The Ripper then raises the mistletoe over Lulu's head and requests the traditional kiss. As she shuts her eyes and presents her lips, the candle flares up. Its gleam reflected in the bread knife on the table holds the Ripper's gaze. He can look at nothing but the shining blade. Long seconds pass as he wrestles, motionless, with his obsession. Finally, leaning forward to consummate the kiss, he grasps the handle of the knife. In the culminating shot, he is facing away from the camera. All we see of Lulu is her right hand, open on his shoulder, pressing him toward her. Suddenly, it clenches hard, then falls, limply dangling, behind his back. We fade to darkness. Nowhere in the cinema has the destruction of beauty been conveyed with more eloquent restraint. As with the killing of Peter Schön, extreme violence is implied, not shown. To paraphrase what Freddy Buache, a Swiss critic, wrote many years later, Lulu's death is in no sense God's judgment on a sinner; she has lived her life in accordance with the high moral imperatives of liberty, and stands in no need of redemption.

After the murder, the Ripper emerges from the building and hurries off into the fog. It is here, in my view, that the film should end. Instead, Pabst moves on to the forlorn figure of Alwa, who stares up at the garret before turning away to follow the Salvation Army procession out of sight. A glib anticlimax indeed, but I'm not sure that I prefer the alternative proposed by Brooks, who has said, with characteristic forthrightness, "The movie should have ended with the knife in the vagina." It may be worth adding that Gustav Diessl, who played the Ripper, was the only man in the cast whom she found sexually appealing. "We just adored each other," she has said in an interview with Richard Leacock, "and I think the final scene was the happiest in the picture. Here he is with a knife he's going to stick up into my interior, and we'd be singing and I'd be doing the Charleston. You wouldn't have known it was a tragic ending. It was more like a Christmas party." At Brooks's request, Pabst had hired a jazz pianist to play between takes, and during these syncopated interludes Brooks and Diessl would often disappear beneath the table to engage in intimate festivities of their own.

The Berlin critics, expecting Lulu to be portrayed as a monster of active depravity, had mixed feelings about Brooks. One reviewer wrote, "Louise Brooks cannot act. She does not suffer. She does nothing." Wedekind himself, however, had said of his protagonist, "Lulu is not a real character but the personification of primitive sexuality, who inspires evil unawares. She plays a purely passive role." Brooks afterward stated her own opinion of what she had achieved. "I played *Pabst's* Lulu," she said, "and she isn't a destroyer of men, like Wedekind's. She's just the same kind of nitwit that I am. Like me, she'd have been an impossible wife, sitting in bed all day reading and drinking gin." Modern critics have elected Brooks's Lulu to a secure place in the movie pantheon. David Thomson describes it as "one of the major female performances in the cinema," to be measured beside such other pinnacles as "Dietrich in the von Sternberg films, Bacall with Hawks, Karina in *Pierrot le Fou*." It is true that in the same list Thomson included Kim Novak in *Vertigo*. It is also true that we are none of us perfect.

Day Two

My first view of the second Pabst–Brooks collaboration, *The Diary of a Lost Girl*, based on *Das Tagebuch einer Verlorenen*, a novel by Margarethe Boehme, and shot in the summer of 1929. After finishing *Pandora,* Brooks had returned to New York and resumed her affair with the millionaire George Marshall. He told her that a new movie company, called RKO and masterminded by Joseph P. Kennedy, was anxious to sign her up for five hundred dollars a week. She replied, "I hate California and I'm not going back." Then Paramount called, ordering her to report for duty on the Coast; it was turning *The Canary Murder Case* into a talkie and required her presence for retakes and dubbing. She refused to go. Under the impression that this was a haggling posture, the studio offered ever vaster sums of money. Brooks's determination remained undented. Goaded to fury, Paramount planted in the columns a petty but damaging little story to the effect that it had been compelled to replace Brooks because her voice was unusable in talkies.

At this point (April 1929), she received a cable from Pabst. It said that he intended to coproduce a French film entitled *Prix de Beauté,* which René Clair would direct, and that they both wanted her for the lead—would she therefore cross the Atlantic as soon as possible? Such was her faith in Pabst that within two weeks she and Clair ("a very small, demure, rather fragile man" is how she afterward described him) were posing together for publicity shots in Paris. When the photographic session was over, Clair escorted her back to her hotel, where he damped her enthusiasm by revealing that he proposed to pull out of the picture forthwith. He advised her to do the same; the production money, he said, simply wasn't there, and might never be. A few days later, he officially retired from the project. (Its place in his schedule was taken by *Sous les Toits de Paris,* which, together with its immediate successors, *Le Million* and *À Nous la Liberté,* established his international reputation.) With nothing to do, and a guaranteed salary of a thousand dollars a week to do it on, Brooks entrained for a spree in Antibes, accompanied by a swarm of rich admirers. When she got back to Paris, Pabst called her from Berlin. *Prix de Beauté,* he said, was postponed; instead, she would star under his direction in *The Diary of a Lost Girl,* at precisely half her present salary. As submissive as ever to her tutor, she arrived in Berlin aboard the next train.

Lovingly photographed by Sepp Allgeier, Brooks in *Lost Girl* is less flamboyant but not less haunting than she is in *Pandora's Box.* The traffic in movie actors traditionally moved westward, from Europe to Hollywood, where their national characteristics were sedulously exploited. Brooks, who was among the few to make the eastbound trip, became in her films with Pabst completely Europeanized. To be more exact: in the context that Pabst prepared for her,

Brooks's American brashness took on an awareness of transience and mortality. The theme of *Lost Girl* is the corruption of a minor—not by sexuality but by an authoritarian society that condemns sexuality. (Pabst must surely have read Wilhelm Reich, the Freudian Marxist, whose theories about the relationship between sexual and political repression were hotly debated in Berlin at the time.) It is the same society that condemns Lulu. In fact, "The Education of Lulu" would make an apt alternative title for *Lost Girl*, whose heroine emerges from her travails ideally equipped for the leading role in *Pandora's Box.* Her name is Thymiane Henning, and she is the sixteen-year-old daughter of a prosperous pharmacist. In the early sequences, Brooks plays her shy and faunlike, peering wide-eyed at a predatory world. She is seduced and impregnated by her father's libidinous young assistant. As soon as her condition is discovered, the double standard swings into action. The assistant retains his job, but, to save the family from dishonor, Thymiane's baby is farmed out to a wet nurse, and she herself is consigned to a home for delinquent girls, run by a bald and ghoulish superintendent and his sadistic wife.

Life in the reformatory is strictly regimented: the inmates exercise to the beat of a drum and eat to the tapping of a metronome. At length, Thymiane escapes from this archetypal hellhole (precursor of many such institutions in subsequent movies, e.g., *Mädchen in Uniform*) and goes to reclaim her baby, only to find that the child has died. Broke and homeless, she meets a street vendor who guides her to an address where food and shelter will be hers for the asking. Predictably, it turns out to be a brothel; far less predictably, even shockingly, Pabst presents it as a place where Thymiane is not degraded but liberated. In the whorehouse, she blossoms, becoming a *fille de joie* in the literal sense of the phrase. Unlike almost any other actress in a similar situation, Brooks neither resorts to pathos nor suggests that there is anything immoral in the pleasure she derives from her new profession. As in *Pandora,* she lives for the moment, with radiant physical abandon. Present love, even for sale, hath present laughter, and what's to come is not only unsure but irrelevant. I agree with Freddy Buache when he says of Brooks's performances with Pabst that they celebrated "the victory of innocence and *amour-fou* over the debilitating wisdom imposed on society by the Church, the Fatherland, and the Family." One of her more outré clients can achieve orgasm only by watching her beat a drum. This ironic echo of life in the reform school is used by Pabst to imply that sexual prohibition breeds sexual aberration. (Even more ironically, the sequence has been censored out of most of the existing prints of the movie.) Brooks is at her best—a happy animal in skintight satin—in a party scene at a night club, where she offers herself as first prize in a raffle. "Pabst wanted realism, so we all had to drink real drinks," she said later. "I played the whole scene stewed on hot, sweet German champagne."

Hereabouts, unfortunately, the film begins to shed its effrontery and to pay lip service to conventional values. Thymiane catches sight of her father across the dance floor; instead of reacting with defiance—after all, he threw her out of his house—she looks stricken with guilt, like the outcast daughter of sentimental fiction. In her absence, Papa has married his housekeeper, by whom he has two children. When he dies, shortly after the nightclub confrontation, he leaves his considerable wealth to Thymiane. Nobly, she gives it all to his penniless widow, so that the latter's offspring "won't have to live the same kind of life as I have." Thereby redeemed, the former whore soon becomes the wife of an elderly aristocrat. Revisiting the reform school, of which she has now been appointed a trustee, she excoriates the staff for its self-righteous cruelties. "A little more kindness," her husband adds, "and no one in the world would ever be lost." Thus lamely, the movie ends.

"Pabst seemed to lose interest," Brooks told an interviewer some years afterward. "He more or less said, 'I'm tired of this picture,' and he gave it a soft ending." His first, and much tougher, intention had been to demonstrate that humanitarianism alone could never solve society's problems. He wanted Thymiane to show her contempt for her husband's liberal platitudes by setting herself up as the madam of a whorehouse. The German distributors, however, refused to countenance such a radical denouement, and Pabst was forced to capitulate. The result is a flawed masterpiece, with a shining central performance that even the closing, compromised sequences cannot dim. Brooks has written that during the making of the film she spent all her off-duty hours with rich revelers of whom Pabst disapproved. On the last day of shooting, "he decided to let me have it." Her friends, he said, were preventing her from becoming a serious actress, and sooner or later they would discard her like an old toy. "Your life is exactly like Lulu's, and you will end the same way," he warned her. The passage of time convinced her that Pabst had a valid point. "Lulu's story," she told a journalist, "is as near as you'll get to mine."

In August 1929, she returned to Paris, where backing had unexpectedly been found for *Prix de Beauté,* her last European movie and her first talkie—although, since she spoke no French, her voice was dubbed. The director, briefly surfacing from obscurity, was Augusto Genina, and René Clair received a credit for the original idea. Like so much of French cinema in the thirties, *Prix de Beauté* is a *film noir*, with wanly tinny music, about a shabby suburban crime of passion. Brooks plays Lucienne, a typist who enters a newspaper beauty contest. It's the kind of role with which one associates Simone Simon, though the rapture that Brooks displays when she wins, twirling with glee as she shows off her presents and trophies, goes well beyond the emotional range accessible to Mlle. Simon. Lucienne-Brooks is triumphantly unliberated; she rejoices in being a beloved, fleshly bauble, and she makes it clear to her husband, a compositor employed by the prize-giving newspaper, that she wants a grander, more snobbish reward for her victory than a visit to a back-street fairground, which is all he has to offer. She leaves him and accepts a part in a film. Consumed by jealousy, he follows her one night to a projection theater in which a rough cut of her movie is being shown. He bursts in and shoots her. As she dies, the French infatuation with irony is fearsomely indulged: her image on the screen behind her is singing the movie's theme song, "Ne Sois Pas Jaloux." In *Prix de Beauté,* Brooks lends her inimitable flair and distinction to a cliché, but it is a cliché nonetheless.

At this point, when Brooks was at the height of her beauty, her career began a steep and bumpy decline. In 1930, she went back to Hollywood, on the strength of a promised contract with Columbia. Harry Cohn, the head of the studio, summoned her to his office for a series of meetings, at each of which he appeared naked from the waist up. Always a plain speaker, he left her in no doubt that good parts would come her way if she responded to his advances. She rebuffed them, and the proffered contract was withdrawn. Elsewhere in Hollywood, she managed to get a job in a feeble two-reel comedy pseudonymously directed by the disgraced Fatty Arbuckle; her old friend Frank Tuttle gave her a supporting role in *It Pays to Advertise* (starring Carole Lombard); and she turned up fleetingly in a Michael Curtiz picture called *God's Gift to Women.* But the word was out that Brooks was difficult and uppity, too independent to suit the system. Admitting defeat, she returned to New York in May 1931. Against her will, but under heavy pressure from George Marshall, her lover and would-be Svengali, she played a small part in *Louder, Please,* a featherweight comedy by Norman Krasna that began its pre-Broadway run in October. After the opening week in Jackson Heights, she was fired by the director, George Abbott. This was her farewell to the theater; it took place on the eve of her twenty-fifth birthday.

For Brooks, as for millions of her compatriots, a long period of unemployment followed. In 1933, determined to break off her increasingly discordant relationship with Marshall, she married Deering Davis, a rich young Chicagoan, but walked out on him after six months of rapidly waning enthusiasm. With a Hungarian partner named Dario Borzani, she spent a year dancing in night clubs, including the Persian Room of the Plaza, but the monotony of cabaret routine dismayed her, and she quit the act in August 1935. That autumn, Pabst suddenly arrived in New York and invited her to play Helen of Troy in a film version of Goethe's *Faust,* with Greta Garbo as Gretchen. Her hopes giddily soared, only to be dashed when Garbo opted out and the project fell through. Once again, she revisited Hollywood, where Republic Pictures wanted to test her for a role in a musical called *Dancing Feet.* She was rejected in favor of a blonde who couldn't dance. "That about did it for me," Brooks wrote later. "From then on, it was straight downhill. And no dough to keep the wolves from the door." In 1936, Universal cast her as the ingénue (Boots Boone) in *Empty Saddles,* a Buck Jones Western, which is the last Brooks movie in the Eastman collection. She looks perplexed, discouraged, and lacking in verve; and her coiffure, with the hair swept back from her forehead, reveals disquieting lines of worry. (Neither she nor Jones is helped by the fact that many of the major sequences of an incredibly complex plot take place at night.) The following year brought her a bit part at Paramount in something called *King of Gamblers,* after which, in her own words, "Harry Cohn gave me a personally conducted tour of hell with no return ticket." Still wounded by her refusal to sleep with him in 1930, Cohn promised her a screen test if she would submit to the humiliation of appearing in the corps de ballet of a Grace Moore musical entitled *When You're in Love.* To his surprise, Brooks accepted the offer—she was too broke to spurn it—and Cohn made sure that the demotion of an erstwhile star was publicized as widely as possible. Grudgingly, he gave her a perfunctory screen test, which he dismissed in two words: "It stunk." In the summer of 1938, Republic hired Brooks to appear with John Wayne (then a minor figure) in *Overland Stage Raiders.* After this low-budget oater, she made no more pictures.

In her entire professional career, Brooks had earned, according to her own calculations, exactly $124,600: $104,500 from films, $10,100 from theater, and $10,000 from all other sources. Not a gargantuan sum, one would think, spread over sixteen years; yet Brooks said to a friend, "I was astonished that it came to so much. But then I never paid any attention to money." In 1940, she left Hollywood for the last time.

EASTMAN HOUSE STANDS in an affluent residential district of Rochester, on an avenue of comparably stately mansions, with broad, tree-shaded lawns. When my second day of séances with Brooks came to an end, I zipped up my notes in a briefcase, thanked the staff of the film department for their help, and departed in a taxi. The driver took me to an apartment building only a few blocks away, where I paid him off. I rode up in the elevator to the third floor and pressed a doorbell a few paces along the corridor. After a long pause, there was a loud snapping of locks. The door slowly opened to reveal a petite woman of fragile build, wearing a woollen bed jacket over a pink nightgown, and holding herself defiantly upright by means of a sturdy metal cane with four rubber-tipped prongs. She had salt-and-pepper hair combed back into a ponytail that hung down well below her shoulders, and she was barefoot. One could imagine this gaunt and elderly child as James Tyrone's wife in *Long Day's Journey into Night,* or, noting the touch of authority and panache in her bearing, as the capricious heroine of Jean Giraudoux's *The Madwoman of Chaillot.* I stated my name, adding that I had an appointment. She nodded and beckoned me in. I greeted her with a respectful embrace. This was my first physical contact with Louise Brooks.

She was seventy-one years old, and until a few months earlier I had thought she was dead. Four decades had passed since her last picture, and it seemed improbable that she had survived such a long period of retirement. Moreover, I did not then know how young she had been at the time of her flowering. Spurred by the TV screening of *Pandora's Box* in January 1978, I had made some inquiries, and soon discovered that she was living in Rochester, virtually bedridden with degenerative osteoarthritis of the hip, and that since 1956 she had written twenty vivid and perceptive articles, mainly for specialist film magazines, on such of her colleagues and contemporaries as Garbo, Dietrich, Keaton, Chaplin, Bogart, Fields, Lillian Gish, ZaSu Pitts, and (naturally) Pabst. Armed with this information, I wrote her a belated fan letter, to which she promptly replied. We then struck up a correspondence, conducted on her side in a bold and expressive prose style. (It matched her handwriting.) Rapport was cemented by telephone calls, which resulted in my visit to Rochester and the date I was now keeping.

She has not left her apartment since 1960, except for a few trips to the dentist and one to a doctor. (She mistrusts the medical profession, and this consultation, which took place in 1976, was her first in thirty-two years.) "You're doing a terrible thing to me," she said as she ushered me in. "I've been killing myself off for twenty years, and you're going to bring me back to life." She lives in two rooms—

modest, spotless, and austerely furnished. From the larger, I remember Venetian blinds, a green sofa, a TV set, a Formica-topped table, a tiny kitchenette alcove, and fleshpink walls sparsely hung with paintings redolent of the twenties. The other room was too small to hold more than a bed (single), a built-in cupboard bursting with press clippings and other souvenirs, a chest of drawers surmounted by a crucifix and a statue of the Virgin, and a stool piled high with books, including works by Proust, Schopenhauer, Ruskin, Ortega y Gasset, Samuel Johnson, Edmund Wilson, and many living authors of serious note. "I'm probably one of the best-read idiots in the world," my hostess said as she haltingly showed me round her domain. Although she eats little (she turns the scale at about eighty-eight pounds), she had prepared for us a perfectly mountainous omelette. Nerves, however, had robbed us of our appetites, and we barely disturbed its mighty silhouette. I produced from my briefcase a bottle of expensive red Burgundy that I had brought as a gift. (Brooks, who used to drink quite heftily, nowadays touches alcohol only on special occasions.) Since she cannot sit upright for long without discomfort, we retired with the wine to her bedroom, where she reclined, sipped, and talked, gesturing fluently, her fingers supple and unclenched. I pulled a chair up to the bedside and listened.

Her voice has the range of a dozen birdcalls, from the cry of a peacock to the fluting of a dove. Her articulation, at whatever speed, is impeccable, and her laughter soars like a kite. I cannot understand why, even if she had not been a beauty, Hollywood failed to realize what a treasure it possessed in the *sound* of Louise Brooks. Like most people who speak memorably, she is highly responsive to vocal nuances in others. She told Kevin Brownlow that her favorite actress ("the person I would be if I could be anyone") was Margaret Sullavan, mainly because of her voice, which Brooks described as "exquisite and far away, almost like an echo," and, again, as "strange, fey, mysterious—like a voice singing in the snow."

My conversations with the Ravishing Hermit of Rochester were spread over several days; for the sake of convenience, I have here compressed them into one session.

She began, at my urging, by skimming through the story of her life since she last faced the Hollywood cameras: "Why did I give up the movies? I could give you seven hundred reasons, all of them true. After I made that picture with John Wayne in 1938, I stayed out on the Coast for two years, but the only people who wanted to see me were men who wanted to sleep with me. Then Walter Wanger warned me that if I hung around any longer I'd become a call girl. So I fled to

Wichita, Kansas, where my family had moved in 1919. But that turned out to be another kind of hell. The citizens of Wichita either resented me for having been a success or despised me for being a failure. And I wasn't exactly enchanted with them. I opened a dance studio for young people, who loved me, because I dramatized everything so much, but it didn't make any money. In 1943, I drifted back to New York and worked for six months in radio soaps. Then I quit, for another hundred reasons, including Wounded Pride of Former Star. [Peal of laughter. Here, as throughout our chat, Brooks betrayed not the slightest trace of self-pity.] During '44 and '45, I got a couple of jobs in publicity agencies, collecting items for Winchell's column. I was fired from both of them, and I had to move from the decent little hotel where I'd been living to a grubby hole on First Avenue at Fifty-ninth Street. That was when I began to flirt with fancies related to little bottles filled with yellow sleeping pills. However, I changed my mind, and in July 1946, the proud, snooty Louise Brooks started work as a salesgirl at Saks Fifth Avenue. They paid me forty dollars a week. I had this silly idea of proving myself 'an honest woman,' but the only effect it had was to disgust all my famous New York friends, who cut me off forever. From then on, I was regarded as a questionable East Side dame. After two years at Saks, I resigned. To earn a little money, I sat down and wrote the usual autobiography. I called it 'Naked on My Goat,' which is a quote from Goethe's *Faust*. In one of the *Walpurgisnacht* scenes, a young witch is bragging about her looks to an old one. 'I sit here naked on my goat,' she says, 'and show my fine young body.' But the old one advises her to wait awhile: 'Though young and tender now, you'll rot, we know, you'll rot.' Then, when I read what I'd written, I threw the whole thing down the incinerator."

Brooks insists that her motive for this act of destruction was *pudeur*. In 1977, she wrote an article for *Focus on Film* headed "Why I Will Never Write My Memoirs," in which she summed herself up as a prototypical Midwesterner, "born in the Bible Belt of Anglo-Saxon farmers, who prayed in the parlor and practiced incest in the barn." Although her sexual education had been conducted in Paris, London, Berlin, and New York, her pleasure was, she wrote, "restricted by the inbred shackles of sin and guilt." Her conclusion was as follows:

In writing the history of a life I believe absolutely that the reader cannot understand the character and deeds of the subject unless he is given a basic understanding of that person's sexual loves and hates and conflicts. It is the only way the reader can make sense out of innumerable apparently senseless

actions. . . . We flatter ourselves when we assume that we have restored the
sexual integrity which was expurgated by the Victorians. It is true that many
exposés are written to shock, to excite, to make money. But in serious books
characters remain as baffling, as unknowable as ever. . . . I too am unwilling
to write the sexual truth that would make my life worth reading. I cannot
unbuckle the Bible Belt.

Accepting a drop more wine, she continued the tale of her wilderness years.
"Between 1948 and 1953, I suppose you could call me a kept woman," she said.
"Three decent rich men looked after me. But then I was *always* a kept woman.
Even when I was making a thousand dollars a week, I would always be paid for
by George Marshall or someone like that. But I never had anything to show for
it—no cash, no trinkets, nothing. I didn't even *like* jewelry—can you imagine?
Pabst once called me a born whore, but if he was right I was a failure, with no
pile of money and no comfortable mansion. I just wasn't equipped to spoil millionaires in a practical, farsighted way. I could live in the present, but otherwise
everything has always been a hundred percent wrong about me. Anyway, the
three decent men took care of me. One of them owned a sheet-metal manufac-
turing company, and the result of that affair is that I am now the owner of the
only handmade aluminum wastebasket in the world. He designed it, and it's in
the living room, my solitary trophy. Then a time came, early in 1953, when my
three men independently decided that they wanted to marry me. I had to escape,
because I wasn't in love with them. As a matter of fact, I've never been in love.
And if I *had* loved a man, could I have been faithful to him? Could he have trusted me beyond a closed door? I doubt it. It was clever of Pabst to know even before
he met me that I possessed the tramp essence of Lulu."
Brooks hesitated for a moment and then went on in the same tone, lightly self-
mocking, "Maybe I should have been a writer's moll. Because when we were talking on the phone, a few Sundays ago, some secret compartment inside me burst,
and I was suddenly overpowered by the feeling of love—a sensation I'd never
experienced with any other man. Are you a variation of Jack the Ripper, who
finally brings me love that I'm prevented from accepting—not by the knife but
by old age? You're a perfect scoundrel, turning up like this and wrecking my gold-
en years! [I was too stunned to offer any comment on this, but not too stunned
to note, with a distinct glow of pride, that Brooks was completely sober.]
Anyhow, to get back to my three suitors, I decided that the only way to avoid

marriage was to become a Catholic, so that I could tell them that in the eyes of the church I was still married to Eddie Sutherland. I went to the rectory of a Catholic church on the East Side, and everything was fine until my sweet, pure religious instructor fell in love with me. I was the first woman he'd ever known who acted like one and treated him like a man. The other priests were furious. They sent him off to California and replaced him with a stern young missionary. After a while, however, even *he* began to hint that it would be a good idea if he dropped by my apartment in the evenings to give me special instruction. But I resisted temptation, and in September 1953, I was baptized a Catholic."

Having paused to light a cigarette, which provoked a mild coughing spasm, Brooks resumed her story. "I almost forgot a strange incident that happened in 1952. Out of the blue, I got a letter from a woman who had been a Cherryvale neighbor of ours. She enclosed some snapshots. One of them showed a nice-looking gray-haired man of about fifty, holding the hand of a little girl—me. On the back she'd written, 'This is Mr. Feathers, an old bachelor who loved kids. He was always taking you to the picture show and buying you toys and candy.' That picture brought back something I'd blacked out of my mind for—what?—thirty-seven years. When I was nine years old, Mr. Feathers molested me sexually. Which forged another link between me and Lulu: when *she* had *her* first lover, she was very young, and Schigolch, the man in question, was middle-aged. I've often wondered what effect Mr. Feathers had on my life. He must have had a great deal to do with forming my attitude toward sexual pleasure. For me, nice, soft, easy men were never enough—there had to be an element of domination—and I'm sure that's all tied up with Mr. Feathers. The pleasure of kissing and being kissed comes from somewhere entirely different, psychologically as well as physically. Incidentally, I told my mother about Mr. Feathers, and—would you believe it? [Peal of laughter.] She blamed *me*! She said I must have led him on. It's always the same, isn't it?" And Brooks ran on in this vein, discussing her sex life openly and jauntily, unbuckling one more notch of the Bible Belt with every sentence she uttered.

The year 1954 was Brooks's nadir. "I was too proud to be a call girl. There was no point in throwing myself into the East River, because I could swim; and I couldn't afford the alternative, which was sleeping pills." In 1955, just perceptibly, things began to look up, and life became once more a tolerable option. Henri Langlois, the exuberant ruler of the Cinémathèque Française, organized in Paris a huge exhibition entitled *Sixty Years of Cinema*. Dominating the entrance hall of the Musée d'Art Moderne were two gigantic blowups, one of the French actress Falconetti in Carl Dreyer's 1928 classic *La Passion de Jeanne d'Arc,* and the other of Brooks in *Pandora's Box.* When a critic demanded to know why he had preferred this nonentity to authentic stars like Garbo and Dietrich, Langlois exploded, "There is no Garbo! There is no Dietrich! There is only Louise Brooks!" In the same year, a group of her friends from the twenties clubbed together to provide a small annuity that would keep her from outright destitution; and she was visited in her Manhattan retreat by James Card, then the curator of film at Eastman House. He had long admired her movies, and he persuaded her to come to Rochester, where so much of her best work was preserved. It was at his suggestion that, in 1956, she settled there.

"Rochester seemed as good a place as any," she told me. "It was cheaper than New York, and I didn't run the risk of meeting people from my past. Up to that time, I had never seen any of my films. And I still haven't—not right through, that is. Jimmy Card screened some of them for me, but that was during my drinking period. I would watch through glazed eyes for about five minutes and sleep through the rest. I haven't even seen *Pandora.* I've been present on two occasions when it was being run, but I was drunk both times. By that I mean I was *navigating* but not *seeing.*" When she watched other people's movies, however, she felt no need for alcoholic sedation. As a working actress, she had never taken films seriously; under Card's tuition, she recognized that the cinema was a valid form of art, and began to develop her own theories about it. In 1956, drawing on her powers of near-total recall, she wrote a study of Pabst for *Image.* This was the first of a sheaf of articles, sharp-eyed and idiosyncratic, that she has contributed over the years to such magazines as *Sight & Sound* (London), *Objectif* (Montreal), *Film Culture* (New York), and *Positif* (Paris).

The Brooks cult burgeoned in 1957, when Henri Langlois crossed the Atlantic to meet her. A year later, he presented "Hommage à Louise Brooks," a festival of her movies that filled the Cinémathèque. The star herself flew to Paris, all expenses paid, and was greeted with wild acclaim at a reception after the Cinémathèque's showing of *Pandora's Box.* (Among those present was Jean-Luc Godard, who paid his own tribute to Brooks in 1962, when he directed *Vivre Sa Vie,* the heroine of which—a prostitute—was played by Anna Karina in an exact replica of the Brooks hairdo. Godard described the character as "a young and pretty Parisian shopgirl who gives her body but retains her soul.") In January 1960, Brooks went to New York and attended a screening of *Prix de Beauté* in the Kaufmann Concert

Hall of the 92nd Street Y, where she made a hilarious little speech that delighted the packed audience. The next day, she returned to Rochester, from which she has never since emerged.

Interviewers and fans occasionally call on her, but for the most part, as she put it to me, "I have lived in virtual isolation, with an audience consisting of the milkman and a cleaning woman." She continued, "Once a week, I would drink a pint of gin, and would become what Dickens called 'gincoherent,' go to sleep, and drowse for four days. That left three days to read, write a bit, and see the odd visitor. No priests, by the way—I said goodbye to the church in 1964. Now and then, there would be a letter to answer. In 1965, for instance, an Italian artist named Guido Crepax started a very sexy and tremendously popular comic strip about a girl called Valentina, who looked exactly like me as Lulu. In fact, she *identified* herself with me. Crepax wrote to thank me for the inspiration and said he regarded me as a twentieth-century myth. I appreciated the tribute and told him that at last I felt I could disintegrate happily in bed with my books, gin, cigarettes, coffee, bread, cheese, and apricot jam. During the sixties, arthritis started to get a grip, and in 1972 I had to buy a medical cane in order to move around. Then, five years ago, the disease really walloped me. My pioneer blood did not pulse through my veins, rousing me to fight it. I collapsed. I took a terrible fall and nearly smashed my hip. That was the end of the booze or any other kind of escape for me. I knew I was in for a bad time, with nothing to face but the absolute meaninglessness of my life. All I've done since then is try to hold the pieces together. And to keep my little squirrel-cage brain distracted."

As an emblematic figure of the twenties, epitomizing the flappers, jazz babies, and dancing daughters of the boom years, Brooks has few rivals, living or dead. Moreover, she is unique among such figures in that her career took her to all the places—New York, London, Hollywood, Paris, and Berlin—where the action was at its height, where experiments in pleasure were conducted with the same zeal (and often by the same people) as experiments in the arts. From her bedroom cupboard Brooks produced an avalanche of manila envelopes, each bulging with mementoes of her halcyon decade. This solitary autodidact, her perceptions deepened by years of immersion in books, looked back for my benefit on the green, gregarious girl she once was, and found much to amuse her. For every photograph she supplied a spoken caption. As she reminisced, I often thought of those Max Beerbohm cartoons that depict the Old Self conversing with the Young Self.

"Here I am in 1922, when I first hit New York, and the label of 'beautiful but dumb' was slapped on me forever. Most beautiful-but-dumb girls think they are smart, and get away with it, because other people, on the whole, aren't much smarter. You can see modern equivalents of those girls on any TV talk show. But there's also a very small group of beautiful women who *know* they're dumb, and this makes them defenseless and vulnerable. They become the Big Joke. I didn't know Marilyn Monroe, but I'm sure that her agonizing awareness of her own stupidity was one of the things that killed her. I became the Big Joke, first on Broadway and then in Hollywood. . . . That's Herman Mankiewicz—an ideal talk-show guest, don't you think, born before his time? In 1925, Herman was trying to educate me, and he invented the Louise Brooks Literary Society. A girl named Dorothy Knapp and I were Ziegfeld's two prize beauties. We had a big dressing room on the fifth floor of the New Amsterdam Theatre building, and people like Walter Wanger and Gilbert Miller would meet there, ostensibly to hear my reviews of books that Herman gave me to read. What they actually came for was to watch Dorothy doing a striptease in front of a full-length mirror. I get some consolation from the fact that, as an idiot, I have provided delight in my time to a very select group of intellectuals. . . . That must be Joseph Schenck. Acting on behalf of his brother Nick, who controlled M-G-M, Joe offered me a contract in 1925 at three hundred a week. Instead, I went to Paramount for two hundred and fifty. Maybe I should have signed with M-G-M and joined what I called the Joe Schenck Mink Club. You could recognize the members at '21' because they never removed their mink coats at lunch. . . . Here's Fritzi LaVerne, smothered in osprey feathers. I roomed with her briefly when we were in the *Follies* together, and she seduced more *Follies* girls than Ziegfeld and William Randolph Hearst combined. That's how I got the reputation of being a lesbian. I had nothing against it in principle, and for years I thought it was fun to encourage the idea. I used to hold hands with Fritzi in public. She had a little Bulgarian boyfriend who was just our height, and we would get into his suits and camp all over New York. Even when I moved out to Yahoo City, California, I could never stop by a lesbian household without being asked to strip and join the happy group baring their operation scars in the sun. But I only loved men's bodies. What maddens me is that because of the lesbian scenes with Alice Roberts in *Pandora* I shall probably go down in film history as one of the gloomy dykes. A friend of mine once said to me, 'Louise Brooks, you're not a lesbian, you're a pansy.' Would you care to decipher that? By the way, are you getting tired of hearing my name?

I'm thinking of changing it. I noticed that there were five people called Brooks in last week's *Variety*. How about June Caprice? Or Louise Lovely?"

I shook my head.

Brooks continued riffling through her collection. "This, of course, is Martha Graham, whose genius I absorbed to the bone during the years we danced together on tour. She had rages, you know, that struck like lightning out of nowhere. One evening when we were waiting to go onstage—I was sixteen—she grabbed me, shook me ferociously, and shouted, 'Why do you ruin your feet by wearing those tight shoes?' Another time, she was sitting sweetly at the makeup shelf pinning flowers in her hair when she suddenly seized a bottle of body makeup and exploded it against the mirror. She looked at the shattered remains for a spell, then moved her makeup along to an unbroken mirror and went on quietly pinning flowers in her hair. Reminds me of the night when Buster Keaton drove me in his roadster out to Culver City, where he had a bungalow on the back lot of M-G-M. The walls of the living room were covered with great glass bookcases. Buster, who wasn't drunk, opened the door, turned on the lights, and picked up a baseball bat. Then, walking calmly round the room, he smashed every pane of glass in every bookcase. Such frustration in that little body! . . . Here, inevitably, are Scott and Zelda. I met them in January 1927, at the Ambassador Hotel in L.A. They were sitting close together on a sofa, like a comedy team, and the first thing that struck me was how *small* they were. I had come to see the genius writer, but what dominated the room was the blazing intelligence of Zelda's profile. It shocked me. It was the profile of a witch. Incidentally, I've been reading Scott's letters, and I've spotted a curious thing about them. In the early days, before Hemingway was famous, Scott always spelled his name wrong, with two 'm's. And when did he start to spell it right? At the precise moment when Hemingway became a bigger star than he was. . . . This is a pool party at somebody's house in Malibu. I know I knock the studio system, but if you were to ask me what it was like to live in Hollywood in the twenties I'd have to say that we were all—oh!— marvelously degenerate and happy. We were a world of our own, and outsiders didn't intrude. People tell you that the reason a lot of actors left Hollywood when sound came in was that their voices were wrong for talkies. That's the official story. The truth is that the coming of sound meant the end of the all-night parties. With talkies, you couldn't stay out till sunrise anymore. You had to rush back from the studios and start learning your lines, ready for the next day's shooting at

8 A.M. That was when the studio machine really took over. It controlled you, mind and body, from the moment you were yanked out of bed at dawn until the publicity department put you back to bed at night."

Brooks paused, silently contemplating revels that ended half a century ago, and then went on. "Talking about bed, here's Tallulah—although I always guessed that she wasn't as keen on bed as everyone thought. And my record for guessing things like that was pretty good. I watched her getting ready for a meeting with a plutocratic boyfriend of hers at the Elysée Hotel. She forgot to wear the emerald ring he'd given her a few days before, but she didn't forget the script of the play she wanted him to produce for her. Her preparations weren't scheming or whorish. Just businesslike. . . . This is a bunch of the guests at Mr. Hearst's ranch, sometime in 1928. The girl with the dark hair and the big smile is Pepi Lederer, one of my dearest friends. She was Marion Davies's niece and the sister of Charlie Lederer, the screenwriter, and she was only seventeen when that picture was taken. My first husband, Eddie Sutherland, used to say that for people who did-n't worship opulence, weren't crazy about meeting celebrities, or didn't need money or advancement from Mr. Hearst, San Simeon was a deadly dull place. I suppose he was right. But when Pepi was there it was always fun. She created a world of excitement and inspiration wherever she went. And I never entered that great dining hall without a shiver of delight. There were medieval banners from Siena floating overhead, and a vast Gothic fireplace, and a long refectory table seating forty. Marion and Mr. Hearst sat with the important guests at the middle of the table. Down at the bottom, Pepi ruled over a group—including me—that she called the Younger Degenerates, and that's where the laughter was. Although Mr. Hearst disapproved of booze, Pepi had made friends with one of the waiters, and we got all the champagne we wanted. She could have been a gifted writer, and for a while she worked for Mr. Hearst's deluxe quarterly *The Connoisseur*, but it was only a courtesy job. Nobody took her seriously, she never learned discipline, and drink and drugs got her in the end. In 1935, she died by jumping out of a window in the psychiatric ward of a hospital in Los Angeles. She was twenty-five years old. Not long ago, I came across her name in the index of a book on Marion Davies, and it broke my heart. Then I remembered a quotation from Goethe that I'd once typed out. I've written it under the photo: 'For a person remains of consequence not so far as he leaves something behind him but so far as he acts and enjoys, and rouses others to action and enjoyment.' That was Pepi."

Of all the names that spilled out of Brooks's memories of America in the twenties, there was one for which she reserved a special veneration: that of Chaplin. In an article for the magazine *Film Culture*, she had described his performances at private parties:

> He recalled his youth with comic pantomimes. He acted out countless scenes for countless films. And he did imitations of everybody. Isadora Duncan danced in a storm of toilet paper. John Barrymore picked his nose and brooded over Hamlet's soliloquy. A Follies girl swished across the room and I began to cry while Charlie denied absolutely that he was imitating me. Nevertheless . . . I determined to abandon that silly walk forthwith.

For me, she filled out the picture. "I was eighteen in 1925, when Chaplin came to New York for the opening of *The Gold Rush*. He was just twice my age, and I had an affair with him for two happy summer months. Ever since he died, my mind has gone back fifty years, trying to define that lovely being from another world. He was not only the creator of the Little Fellow, though that was miracle enough. He was a self-made aristocrat. He taught himself to speak cultivated English, and he kept a dictionary in the bathroom at his hotel so that he could learn a new word every morning. While he dressed, he prepared his script for the day, which was intended to adorn his private portrait of himself as a perfect English gentleman. He was also a sophisticated lover, who had affairs with Peggy Hopkins Joyce and Marion Davies and Pola Negri, and he was a brilliant businessman, who owned his films and demanded fifty percent of the gross—which drove Joe Schenck wild, along with all the other people who were plotting to rob him. Do you know, I can't once remember him *still*? He was always standing up as he sat down, and going out as he came in. Except when he turned off the lights and went to sleep, without liquor or pills, like a child. Meaning to be bitchy, Herman Mankiewicz said, 'People never sat at his feet. He went to where people were sitting and stood in front of them.' But how we paid attention! We were hypnotized by the beauty and inexhaustible originality of this glistening creature. He's the only genius I ever knew who spread himself equally over his art and his life. He loved showing off in fine clothes and elegant phrases—even in the witness box. When Lita Grey divorced him, she put about vile rumors that he had a depraved passion for little girls. He didn't give a damn, even though people said his career would be wrecked. It still infuriates me that he never defended himself against any of those ugly lies, but the truth is that he existed on a plane above pride, jealousy, or hate. I never heard him say a snide thing about anyone. *He lived totally without fear.* He knew that Lita Grey and her family were living in his house in Beverly Hills, planning to ruin him, yet he was radiantly carefree—happy with the success of *The Gold Rush* and with the admirers who swarmed around him. Not that he *exacted* adoration. Even during our affair, he knew that I didn't adore him in the romantic sense, and he didn't mind at all. Which brings me to one of the dirtiest lies he allowed to be told about him: that he was mean with money. People forget that Chaplin was the only star ever to keep his ex–leading lady [Edna Purviance] on his payroll for life, and the only producer to pay his employees their full salaries even when he wasn't in production. When our joyful summer ended, he didn't give me a fur from Jaeckel or a bangle from Cartier, so that I could flash them around, saying, 'Look what I got from Chaplin.' The day after he left town, I got a nice check in the mail, signed Charlie. And then I didn't even write him a thank-you note. Damn me."

Brooks's souvenirs of Europe, later in the twenties, began with pictures of a burly, handsome, dark-haired man, usually alighting from a train: George Preston Marshall, the millionaire who was her frequent bedfellow and constant adviser between 1927 and 1933. "If you care about *Pandora's Box,* you should be grateful to George Marshall," she told me. "I'd never heard of Mr. Pabst when he offered me the part. It was George who insisted that I should accept it. He was passionately fond of the theater and films, and he slept with every pretty show-business girl he could find, including all my best friends. George took me to Berlin with his English valet, who stepped off the train blind drunk and fell flat on his face at Mr. Pabst's feet."

The Brooks collection contains no keepsakes of the actress whom she pipped at the post in the race to play Lulu, and of whom, when I raised the subject, she spoke less than charitably. "Dietrich? That *contraption!* She was one of the beautiful-but-dumb girls, like me, but she belonged to the category of those who thought they were smart and fooled other people into believing it. But I guess I'm just being insanely jealous, because I know she's a friend of yours—isn't she?" By way of making amends, she praised Dietrich's performance as Lola in *The Blue Angel,* and then, struck by a sudden thought, interrupted herself: "Hey! Why don't I ask Marlene to come over from Paris? We could work on our memoirs together. Better still, she could write mine, and I hers—'Lulu' by Lola, and 'Lola' by Lulu."

To put it politely, however, Dietrich does not correspond to Brooks's ideal image of a movie goddess. But who does—apart from Margaret Sullavan, whose voice, as we know, she reveres? A few months after our Rochester encounter, she sent me a letter that disclosed another, unexpected object of her admiration. In it she said:

> I've just been listening to Toronto radio. There was a press conference with Ava Gardner, who is making a movie in Montreal. Her beauty has never excited me, and I have seen only one of her films, *The Night of the Iguana*, in which she played a passive role that revealed her power of stillness but little else. On radio, sitting in a hotel room, triggered by all the old stock questions, she said nothing new or stirring—just "Sinatra could be very nice or very rotten—get me another drink, baby—I made fifty-four pictures and the only part I understood was in *The Snows of Kilimanjaro*. . . . " In her conversation, there was nothing about great acting or beauty or sex, and no trace of philosophical or intellectual concern. Yet for the first time in my life I was proud of being a movie actress, unmixed with theater art. Ava is in essence what I think a movie star should be: a beautiful person with a unique, mysterious personality unpolluted by Hollywood. And she is so *strong*. She did not have to run away (like Garbo) to keep from being turned into a product of the machine. . . . What I should like to know is whether, as I sometimes fancy, I ever had a glimmer of that quality of integrity which makes Ava shine with her own light.

The next picture out of the manila envelopes showed Brooks, inscrutable and somewhat forlorn in a sequined evening gown, sitting at a table surrounded by men with pencil-thin mustaches who were wearing tuxedos, black ties, and wing collars. These men were all jabbering into telephones and laughing maniacally. None of them were looking at Brooks. Behind them I could make out oak-paneled walls and an out-of-focus waiter with a fish-eyed stare and a strong resemblance to Louis Jouvet. "You know where that was taken, of course," Brooks said.

I was sorry, but I didn't.

"That's Joe Zelli's!" she cried. "Zelli's was the most famous nightclub in Paris. I can't remember all the men's names, but the one on the extreme right used to drink ether. The one on my left was half Swedish and half English. I lived with him in several hotels. Although he was very young, he had snow-white hair, so we always called him the Eskimo. The fellow next to him, poor guy, was killed the very next day. He was cut to pieces by a speedboat propeller at Cannes."

Whenever I think of the twenties, I shall see that flashlit hysterical tableau at Zelli's and the unsmiling seraph at the center of it.

From the fattest of all her files, Brooks now pulled out a two-shot. Beaming in a cloche hat, she stands arm in arm with a stocky, self-possessed man in a homburg. He also wears steel-rimmed glasses, a bow tie, and a well-cut business suit; you would guess he was in his early forties. "Mr. Pabst," she said simply. "That was 1928, in Berlin, while we were making *Pandora's Box.* As I told you, I arrived with George Marshall, and Mr. Pabst hated him, because he kept me up all night, going round the clubs. A few weeks later, George went back to the States, and after that Mr. Pabst locked me up in my hotel when the day's shooting was finished. Everyone thought he was in love with me. On the rare evenings when I went to his apartment for dinner, his wife, Trudi, would walk out and bang the door. Mr. Pabst was a highly respectable man, but he had the most extraordinary collection of obscene stills in the world. He even had one of Sarah Bernhardt nude with a black-lace fan. Did you know that in the twenties it was the custom for European actresses to send naked pictures of themselves to movie directors? He had all of them. Anyway, I didn't have an affair with him in Berlin. In 1929, though, when he was in Paris trying to set up *Prix de Beauté,* we went out to dinner at a restaurant and I behaved rather outrageously. For some reason, I slapped a close friend of mine across the face with a bouquet of roses. Mr. Pabst was horrified. He hustled me out of the place and took me back to my hotel, where—what do I do? I'm in a *terrific* mood, so I decide to banish his disgust by giving the best sexual performance of my career. I jump into the hay and deliver myself to him body and soul. [Her voice is jubilant.] He acted as if he'd never experienced such a thing in his life. You know how men want to pin medals on themselves when they excite you? They get positively radiant. Next morning, Mr. Pabst was so pleased he couldn't see straight. That was why he postponed *Prix de Beauté* and arranged to make *The Diary of a Lost Girl* first. He wanted the affair to continue. But I didn't, and when I got to Berlin it was like *Pandora's Box* all over again, except that this time the man I brought with me was the Eskimo—my white-headed boy from Zelli's."

Brooks laughed softly, recalling the scene. "Mr. Pabst was there at the station to meet me. He was appalled when I got off the train with the Eskimo. On top of that, I had a wart on my neck, and Esky had just slammed the compartment door on my finger. Mr. Pabst took one stark look at me, told me I had to start work the next morning, and dragged me away to a doctor, who burned off the wart. If you study the early sequences of *Lost Girl,* you can see the sticking plaster on my neck. I hated to hurt Mr. Pabst's feelings with the Eskimo, but I simply could not bring myself to repeat that one and only night. The irony, which Mr. Pabst never knew, was that although Esky and I shared a hotel suite in Berlin, we didn't sleep together until much later, when *Lost Girl* was finished and we were spending a few days in Paris. 'Eskimo,' I said to him the evening before we parted, 'this is the night.' And it was— another first and last for Brooks."

MORE FRAGMENTS OF BROOKSIANA:

I: Do you think there are countries that produce particularly good lovers?
BROOKS: Englishmen are the best. And priest-ridden Irishmen are the worst.

I: What are your favorite films?
BROOKS: *An American in Paris, Pygmalion,* and *The Wizard of Oz.* Please don't be disappointed.
I: They're all visions of wish fulfillment. An American at large with a gamine young dancer in a fantasy playground called Paris. A Cockney flower girl who becomes the toast of upper-class London. And a child from your home state who discovers, at the end of a trip to a magic world, that happiness was where she started out.
BROOKS: You *are* disappointed.
I: Not a bit. They're first-rate movies, and they're all aspects of you.

Postscript from a letter Brooks wrote to me before we met: "Can you give me a reason for sitting here in this bed, going crazy, with not one god-damned excuse for living?" I came up with more than one reason; viz., (a) to receive the homage of those who cherish the images she has left on celluloid; (b) to bestow the pleasure of her conversation on those who seek her company; (c) to appease her hunger for gleaning wisdom from books; and (d) to test the truth of a remark she had made to a friend: "The Spanish philosopher Ortega y Gasset once said, 'We are all lost creatures.' It is only when we admit this that we have a chance of finding ourselves."

DESPITE THE NUMEROUS MEN who have crossed the trajectory of her life, Brooks has pursued her own course. She has flown solo. The price to be paid for such individual autonomy is, inevitably, loneliness, and her loneliness is prefigured in one of the most penetrating comments she has ever committed to print: "The great art of films does not consist in descriptive movement of face and body, but in the movements of thought and soul transmitted in a kind of intense isolation."

As I ROSE TO LEAVE her apartment, she gave me a present: a large and handsome volume entitled *Louise Brooks—Portrait d'une Anti-Star*. Published in Paris in 1977, it contained a full pictorial survey of her career, together with essays, critiques, and poems devoted to her beauty and talent. She inscribed it to me, and copied out, beneath her signature, the epitaph she has composed for herself: "I never gave away anything without wishing I had kept it; nor kept anything without wishing I had given it away." The book included an account by Brooks of her family background, which I paused to read. It ended with this paragraph, here reproduced from her original English text:

> Over the years I suffered poverty and rejection and came to believe that my mother had formed me for a freedom that was unattainable, a delusion. Then . . . I was . . . confined to this small apartment in this alien city of Rochester. . . . Looking about, I saw millions of old people in my situation, wailing like lost puppies because they were alone and had no one to talk to. But they had become enslaved by habits which bound their lives to warm bodies that talked. I was free! Although my mother had ceased to be a warm body in 1944, she had not forsaken me. She comforts me with every book I read. Once again I am five, leaning on her shoulder, learning the words as she reads aloud *Alice in Wonderland*.

She insisted on getting out of bed to escort me to the door. We had been talking earlier of Proust, and she had mentioned his maxim that the future could never be predicted from the past. Out of her past, I thought, in all its bizarre variety, who knows what future she may invent? "Another thing about Proust," she said, resting on her cane in the doorway. "No matter how he dresses his characters up in their social disguises, we always know how they look naked." As we know it, I reflected, in Brooks's performances.

I kissed her goodbye, buttoned up my social disguise—for it was a chilly evening—and joined the other dressed-up people on the streets of Rochester.

LULU IN HOLLYWOOD

The Brooks family were poor English farmers who came to America on a merchant ship at the end of the eighteenth century. They settled in the mountainous northeastern part of Tennessee. During the Civil War, they fought against the slaveholders who owned plantations in western Tennessee. In 1871, my great-grandfather John Brooks, with his son Martin and Martin's young family, journeyed by covered wagon a thousand miles across Tennessee, Arkansas, and the corner of Missouri to homestead in the southeastern part of the free state of Kansas. The government let them have one hundred and sixty acres of land near the village of Burden. There they built a log cabin, ten feet by twelve, in which all twelve members of the family had to live. The Pawnee and Cherokee Indians had already been driven into a reservation in the Oklahoma Territory, to the south, while the last of the Plains Indians were then fighting hopelessly against the United States Army and Cavalry, which soon swept their survivors west into Colorado. Furthermore, by 1875 the Indians' subsistence—the millions of buffalo—had been slaughtered by the white hunters. Thereafter, homesteaders poured in.

My father, Leonard Porter Brooks, who was the second of eight children, was born in 1868, before the family left Tennessee. He became a lawyer, and in 1904, at the age of thirty-six, married my mother, Myra Rude, who was nineteen. They moved to the little town of Cherryvale, Kansas, where Father worked for the Prairie Oil Company until it was gobbled up by John D. Rockefeller. Mother bore four children: Martin, in 1905; Louise, in 1906; Theodore, in 1912; and June, in 1914.

A small, black-haired man, quiet, cheerful, and energetic, my father had only two loves throughout his life—my mother and his law practice. He dreamed of becoming a United States district judge—an unrealizable dream, because his abhorrence of boozing, whoring, and profanity made him unacceptable to the rough politicians of his day. In 1919, we moved to Wichita, where my father had a general law practice and where a common joke was that "L. P. Brooks is so honest that his secretary makes more money than he does." However, when he was nearly eighty, his integrity was rewarded by his being made an assistant attorney general of the state of Kansas. He died in 1960, at the age of ninety-two.

My mother was born in Burden, Kansas, in 1884, to Mary and Thomas Rude, who was a country doctor. Because he was the only doctor for miles around, the villagers, though they were a puritanical lot, found it necessary to condone much in him that they would never have forgiven in others—drinking, smoking, swearing, and refusing to go to church. He delivered babies, set bones, and eased the pain of the dying with morphine. When the weather was good, he drove to see his patients in a horse-and-buggy. When the weather was bad, he rode horseback. And when the weather was very bad and the horse could not find its way in the snowdrifts, he went on foot. A few of the patients paid him with money, some with pigs or sacks of corn, many with nothing at all.

As the eldest of six children borne by a tiny, withdrawn mother who "enjoyed poor health," Myra Rude had been forced to sacrifice her girlhood to the care of what she called "squalling brats." When she married, she told Father that he was her escape to freedom and the arts, and that any squalling brats she produced could take care of themselves. And that is what happened. My mother pursued freedom by writing book reviews to present at her women's club, by delivering lectures on Wagner's *Ring*, and by playing the piano, at which she was extremely talented. When my older brother and I got into a fight, my father would retire to his lawbooks and violin on the third floor, and my mother, who had a sense of the absurd which almost always reduced crime and punishment to laughter, often simply laughed. She did, however, foster my dancing career. It began when I was ten; both my mother and I hoped I would become a serious dancer. From the time I was ten, when a Mrs. Buckpitt came eight miles by train from the town of Independence to the village of Cherryvale to give me dancing lessons, I was what amounted to a professional dancer. I danced at men's clubs, women's clubs, fairs, and various other gatherings in southeastern Kansas. I was given to temper tantrums, brought on by an unruly costume or a wrong dance tempo, but my mother, who was my costumer and pianist, bore them with professional calm. My father thought I had been mutilated when Mother, in the interests of improving my stage appearance, had a barber chop off my long black braids and shape what remained of my hair in a straight Dutch bob with bangs. He called my dancing career "just silly."

After we moved to Wichita, however, I studied dancing at the Wichita College of Music, with Alice Campbell, who also taught elocution, a fancy exercise in speech which permitted her—she was from Kansas City, Missouri— to express her disdain for the entire state of Kansas. (I later learned that every state in the Union, with the exception of Nebraska, felt disdain for Kansas.) In the twenties, Isadora Duncan, Ruth St. Denis, and Ted Shawn were just beginning to give a teachable form to serious American dance. For the rest, dancing teachers around the country taught the high kicks, splits, and cart-

wheels of acrobatic dancing; or tap dancing; or a flabby imitation of the technique of the Russian ballet. Miss Campbell, her plump body uniformed in a
starched white middy, pleated black serge bloomers, black hose, and ballet
slippers, turned out her toes in the five positions, raised her legs in arabesques,
pirouetted with ladylike care. Her regional superiority could not approximate
my contempt for her brazen counterfeit of an art—revealed to all Wichita
when the Pavley-Oukrainsky Ballet, of Chicago, appeared with the annual
Wheat Show in 1920.

Here I must confess to a lifelong curse. In December, 1940, Scott Fitzgerald
touched it when he wrote to his daughter, Scotty, "Zelda is tragically brilliant
in all matters except that of central importance—she has failed as a social
creature." On first meeting Ernest Hemingway, in 1925, Zelda called him
"bogus." Hemingway retaliated by publicizing her as "crazy" and Scott as a
destructive drunk, with the result that they were banished by their friends the
Gerald Murphys and consequently by the rest of the social colony on the
French Riviera. A year later, my friend Townsend Martin, a screenwriter at
Paramount who had gone to Princeton with Fitzgerald, and who spent a part
of each summer in Paris and Antibes, gave me my first insight into the herd
mentality of high society. Returning from France in 1926, he declared that
the conduct of his previously adored Fitzgeralds "has become too outrageous,"
and went on to say, "Nobody sees them anymore." As for my own failure as a
social creature, my mother did attempt to make me less openly critical of
people's false faces. "Now, dear, try to be more popular," she told me. "Try
not to make people so mad!" I would watch my mother, pretty and charming,
as she laughed and made people feel clever and pleased with themselves, but
I could not act that way. And so I have remained, in cruel pursuit of truth
and excellence, an inhumane executioner of the bogus, an abomination to all
but those few who have overcome their aversion to truth in order to free whatever is good in them.

Inevitably, the time came when Miss Campbell dismissed me from her
dancing class, saying that I was spoiled, bad-tempered, and insulting. It was
useless for Mother to plead, "Yes, Louise *is* hard on everyone, but she is *much*
harder on herself"; Miss Campbell had borne the intensity of my critical stare
for the last time. My 1921 diary records, "Although Mother has gone to
everybody, weeping and telling the tale, it has left me with a curiously relieved
feeling. I must study, and that means away to broader fields. I've had enough

of teaching my teacher what to teach me." It didn't occur to Mother that her little monster had taken shape in her own happy home, where truth was never punished. Away from his law office and the courts, my father, a peaceable man, avoided litigation at home with his children. He, like my mother, often turned our naughty deeds into jokes. At the dinner table once, when Martin confessed to having thrown me down the steep back stairs, Father suggested that next time it would be safer to throw me down to the first landing of the U-shaped front stairs. My mother nearly always had more creative uses for her energy than disciplining children. One day, while she was seated at the piano, I ran to her to confess that I had just smashed a cup belonging to her best set of Haviland china. Without looking at me, she said, "Now, dear, don't bother me when I am memorizing Bach." Never having experienced the necessity for lying at home, I went into the world with an established habit of truthfulness, which has automatically eliminated from my life the boring sameness that must be experienced by liars. All lies are alike. My parents' resolute pursuit of their own interests also accounted for my own early autonomy and my later inability, when I went to work in the Hollywood film factories, to submit to slavery.

My father and mother were examples of excellence. In his attic office, filled with calfbound lawbooks, Father worked on his briefs. At the piano, Mother spent hours mastering the difficult timing of Debussy, a composer new to the prairie in 1920. It was by watching her face that I first recognized the joy of creative effort.

The unsolved mystery of my mother's character was why, although she was such a talented pianist, she never played as a soloist in public. She gave her Wagner lectures on *The Ring;* she gave her book reviews; she even played onstage for my dances. Yet never in her sixty years of life did she so much as appear in a piano recital on her own, nor did she ever offer any reason for obscuring her art. I can still see her, in 1931, inspecting the grand piano left behind by the band leader Paul Whiteman when he rented me his Hollywood house. "My goodness, Louise, there has been enough liquor spilled in this piano to set it afloat," she said. "It can't possibly be tuned." I would gladly have rented a decent piano if she had expressed a wish for one, but she did not, and she didn't complain about doing without one for the six months we lived in Whiteman's house.

Blacklisted by Miss Campbell, I was without a dancing teacher when, in November, 1921, Ted Shawn, assisted by Martha Graham, Betty May, and

Charles Weidman, appeared in a dance recital at the Crawford Theatre. After the performance, Mother took me backstage to meet Mr. Shawn. He told us that he was on his way to open a dance school in New York, and that I should come there for the summer course in 1922. Although Father loved Mother as much as he loved his law practice, it took all winter and spring for her to wheedle him into providing the Denishawn tuition of three hundred dollars, and the expense money for my summer in New York. She finally overcame his strong objection to sending "a little fifteen-year-old girl away from home alone" by finding me a chaperon, Alice Mills, a stocky, bespectacled housewife of thirty-six who, having fallen idiotically in love with the beautiful Ted Shawn at first sight, decided to study dance with him. She agreed to accompany me on the train and live with me in New York.

So it was that in the summer of 1922 poor Mrs. Mills found herself next to my hot, restless body in a double bed in a rented room in a railroad flat in a building on Eighty-sixth Street near Riverside Drive. Denishawn classes were held in the basement of a church on Broadway near Seventy-second Street. Mr. Shawn's lessons consisted of demonstrations of his matchless balance and body control in such creations as his *Japanese Spear Dance* and his *Pose Plastique*. Charles Weidman, his most experienced male dancer, took us through barre and ballet exercises. During a sweltering July and August, I went to weekday classes from ten to twelve in the morning and from one to three in the afternoon. Even in the ballet work, we danced barefoot, which was painful for unaccustomed feet on the splintering pine floor. Having gone barefoot during Kansas summers, I was spared the torn soles and blisters that tormented some of the pupils. Sweat! Sweat! Sweat! Exhausted boys stood in pools of their own sweat. Unwashed black wool bathing suits stank with stale sweat. The only sweat-free, stink-free pupil was also the only New York pupil—a sweet, lonely fat girl, who stood around waiting for one of the three boys in the class to ask her out, which none of them ever did. Most of the students were females from the Middle West, to which, like my chaperon, Alice Mills, they would return to establish Denishawn schools. Kansas-born though I was, "these hicks," with their marcelled hair, their blouses and skirts, and their flat, unsyncopated voices describing the wonders of Grant's Tomb and the Statue of Liberty, filled me with scorn.

I tolerated Mrs. Mills' provincialism because she shared my love of the theatre. Together, we saw all the Broadway shows, one of them being a favorite of mine—the *Ziegfeld Follies*. In the first act, Fanny Brice's burlesque of Pavlova's swan dance filled the New Amsterdam Theatre with laughter. In the last act, standing motionless in front of a black velvet curtain, with black velvet sheathing her exquisite figure, she broke the audience's heart with her singing of "My Man." (Three years later, I would hear this art of transmitting emotion by phrasing alone echoed in the voice of Helen Morgan singing Gershwin's "The Man I Love.") The rest of my attention was concentrated on the famous *Follies* girls. I was not impressed. Only Anastasia Reilly, with her smooth dark hair and her boyish figure set off by a pageboy costume, showed personality, that faithfulness to nature which I sought, and still seek, in all human beings. The rest of the girls wore smiles as fixed as their towering feather headdresses. I decided right then that onstage I would never smile unless I felt like it. For inside the brat who sweated four hours a day at dancing school lived the secret bride of New York whose goal was the sophisticated grace of the lovely women already seen and studied in the pages of *Harper's Bazaar* and *Vanity Fair*. In Wichita, Mother had permitted me to subscribe to those expensive magazines—magazines that so infuriated my jealous brother Martin that he would tear them up and hide the scraps behind the bookcases in the living room.

Our house back in Wichita—a fourteen-room gray frame structure—was literally falling down with books. The foundation on the right side had sunk eleven inches from the weight of the lawbooks in Father's third-floor retreat. There were new books in the bedrooms, old books in the basement, and unread books in the living room; and in the library were the books I loved. Father's was basically an English Victorian library, stocked with Dickens, Thackeray, Tennyson, Carlyle, John Stuart Mill, and Darwin. Among the American authors were Emerson, Hawthorne, and Mark Twain. Goethe was the only foreign-language genius represented. All these books I read with delight, not caring in the least that I understood little of what I read. My passion for words was born when, at the age of five, I learned to read by looking over Mother's shoulder as she read *A Child's Garden of Verses* and *Alice in Wonderland* aloud. Mother herself laughed at literature. For her book reviews, she selected such books as *Nijinsky*, written by the dancer's wife, Romola. Its strange sexual overtones set up a pleasurable creaking of the respectable matrons' chairs. Behind their backs, putting on her club-member's face, Mother would coo unctuously, "Myra Brooks is *so* cultured."

Culture, I was to learn, was not a prerequisite for becoming a sophisticated New Yorker. It was, in fact, a handicap. The rich men who before long were exhibiting me in fashionable restaurants, theatres, and nightclubs shrank like truant schoolboys from the name of Shakespeare, and they looked upon an evening spent at the Metropolitan Opera or at a concert in Carnegie Hall as unthinkable misery. Since I could not gossip about these socialites' families and friends, did not feel secure discussing the theatre and movies, and detested the vulgar game of dirty jokes and sexual innuendos, I talked scarcely at all. Years later, the dress designer Travis Banton told me that in 1925, at the Colony—the grandest restaurant in town—he watched from another table and put me in the category of "beautiful but dumb," where I remained to the end of my film career.

In 1922, then, if I was to create my dream woman, I had to get rid of my Kansas accent, to learn the etiquette of the social élite, and to learn to dress beautifully. I could not correct my speech at a fashionable girls' school. I could not learn table manners from escorts embarrassed by my social inferiority. I could not afford Fifth Avenue couturiers. Therefore, I went for my education directly to the unknown people who were experts in such matters—the people at the bottom whose services supported the enchantment at the top of New York. My English instructor was a fresh, contemptuous soda jerk at a Broadway drugstore where I went for fudge sundaes. Because he was working his way through Columbia University, because he spoke excellent English and had a fine ear for my accent, which he mimicked, I refused to let him drive me away in anger. I did not possess the appeal of a child star, but I possessed a more powerful attraction: a pupil's total attention. Nobody can learn to dance without complete attention and sustained concentration on the disposition of the head, neck, trunk, arms, legs, and feet—on the use of every muscle of the body as it moves before the eyes with the speed of motion-picture film. And not even an unwilling teacher can resist the flattery of extraordinarily close attention. One day, when the soda jerk was making the customers at the fountain laugh with a story about "mulking a kee-yow," I stopped him, saying, "Instead of making fun of me, why don't you teach me how to say it?" While he was concocting a banana split, he began to smile at the fancy of becoming my Pygmalion, and before I finished my fudge sundae our lessons had begun. "Mulk" became "milk," and "kee-yow" became "cow." Then: "Not 'watter' as in 'hotter' but 'water' as in 'daughter.'"

And it's not 'hep,' you hayseed—it's 'help,' 'help,' 'help'!" Within a month of fudge sundaes, this boy had picked his way through my vocabulary, eliminating the last trace of my hated Kansas accent. From the start, it had been my intention not to exchange one label for another. I didn't want to speak the affected London stage-English of the high-comedy stars, like Ina Claire and Ruth Chatterton; I wanted to speak clean, unlabeled English. My soda jerk spoke clean, unlabeled English. Mother had already lowered my childish squeals to a pleasant middle range, making me forever aware of the voice as a manipulative power.

I went on tour with Ruth St. Denis, Ted Shawn, and the Denishawn Dancers for the 1922–23 season, after which I attended a Denishawn summer school at Mariarden, a summer-theatre-school-camp near Peterborough, New Hampshire. There I became a friend of Barbara Bennett, the seventeen-year-old daughter of Richard Bennett, the famous actor. In September, when we returned to New York—Barbara to her home, I to rehearse for a second season on tour—she introduced me to the Wall Street brokers who would take me to dine at the Colony. And there I, who in Kansas had never seen a lobster, was terrorized by a bright-red lobster, which I sent away uneaten. When I questioned Barbara about lobsters, she said, "You just mess them around in butter and eat them, silly." At the Forty-second Street Public Library, after an unsuccessful hour with Emily Post's *Etiquette*, I read an advertisement in a magazine for Nelson Doubleday's *Book of Etiquette* which exactly described my plight. It showed a girl staring wild-eyed at a menu and said, "Across the table her escort smiles at her, proud of her prettiness, glad to notice that others admire, then, with surprise, he gives the waiter her order for a chicken salad. This was the third time she had ordered chicken salad while dining with him. He would think she didn't know how to order a dinner, didn't know how to pronounce those French words on the menu, didn't know how to use the table appointments as gracefully as she would have liked. Well, did she? No." That book taught me nothing, either. Evidently, I had to learn by direct contact with my instructor.

A few nights later, when I was sawing away at a squab at the Colony, it scooted off my plate. One of the captains, Ernest, whisked it away and returned with a fresh squab, which I watched him carve on the service table. From then on, indifferent to the reactions of my dinner partners, I took instructions from the waiters on how to eat everything on the menu. There was how-to-bone-a-brook-trout night, how-to-fork-snails night, how-to-dismember-artichokes night, and so on, until we came to the bottom of the menu, which included a dessert of the understanding and proper pronunciation of French words. At the dinner following my graduation, I announced to Ernest that I was at last going to order a dish I truly liked—creamed chipped beef. He sent a busboy to a Madison Avenue delicatessen for a jar of chipped beef, which was transformed into the most delicious chipped-beef-in-cream-on-toast I would ever eat.

Mrs. Bennett, the actress Adrienne Morrison, had sent Barbara to Mariarden in the hope that exercise would strengthen her long, flat feet and her long, slim legs. She shared a cabin with me and two other girls, with whom she never became friendly. She became my friend because my strange customs made her laugh. In the dining hall, she sat next to me at one of a row of long tables upon which were served what she referred to as "those disgusting country breakfasts." After several mornings of sipping coffee, nibbling toast, and watching me devour big slabs of apple pie, she began our friendship by smiling at me and saying, "Hello, Pie Face." From then on, I participated in her efforts to inject some excitement into her bored existence. Defying the nine-o'clock lights-out regulation, she invited Peterborough boys to our cabin. They brought us cigarettes and applejack. In return, although she permitted no sexual liberties, Barbara entertained the boys with an enviable collection of dirty songs and limericks. I can still remember every word of:

> In Fairy Town,
> In Fairy Town,
> They don't go up,
> They all go down.
> Even the chief of police is queer.
> Oophs, my dear,
> Listen here,
> The elevator's there they say.
> They don't go up,
> Just the other way.
> Holy Bejesus,
> There's lots of paresis
> In Fairy Town.

As she became aware of my dangerous ignorance of sexual matters and my offensive social behavior, Barbara, for perhaps the only time in her passionate, reckless life, exerted herself in another's behalf: she faced down family and friends in order to protect and instruct "that obnoxious little Brooks girl." My education in the art of dress did not begin until I returned to New York in September. Denishawn rehearsals left me plenty of time to visit the Bennett apartment on Park Avenue. One morning, the apartment door was opened by Mrs. Bennett. She looked at me as if I were a stray dog, and said, "What are you doing here at eight o'clock in the morning?" I began to cry, so she let me in and left me on a sofa, waiting for Barbara to wake up. In a gray wrapper, without makeup, how worn and unhappy Mrs. Bennett looked. Not a bit like her elegant fashion photographs in *Vogue*. And this beautiful living room was her creation—all white with dark touches, uncluttered, like a Chinese painting. It bore no resemblance to the usual crowded rooms of the rich, which repelled me. Yet, like Mrs. Bennett, the room had the look of something uncared-for and unloved.

After a while, Barbara's beautiful younger sister, Joan, came in with her schoolbooks to study at the secretary by the window. Barbara's beautiful older sister, Constance, had just started her career, but her reputation as the best-dressed and haughtiest actress in movies was already established. All the girls had Richard Bennett's wide cheekbones and finely set eyes, but in character the three daughters did not resemble one another in any way. Constance loved money. During a career that continued to the year of her death, in 1965, she demanded and received a salary equal to that of the top stars. Yet beauty, great acting ability, and a lovely voice could not compensate for the lack of the one attribute without which the rest did not matter: she did not have that generosity, that love for her audience, which makes a true star. What Joan loved was security. Her marriages to men powerful in films guaranteed a successful career. Barbara made a career of her emotions. Periods of work or marriage were terminated by her frightening, abandoned laughter of despair and failure. Only her death, in 1958, achieved in her fifth suicide attempt, could be termed a success. In the dusty white living room, Joan, who was always kind to me, was putting on her glasses to study her history book. "What I can't figure out," I said, "is how, if you can't see without your glasses, you get around without them." Joan took them off and smiled at me. "I can see something without them. For instance, your long black dress. Where did you get that funny, old-lady's dress?"

"A woman in a shop on Broadway sold it to me."

Joan laughed.

At eleven, we heard sounds of rising Bennetts. We heard Constance raging at Barbara: "If you dare to sneak out once more in my white chiffon, I am going to slit your throat." We heard Richard Bennett singing, "I love life and I want to live," followed by his entrance in a blue brocade dressing gown for a trip to the liquor cabinet. After tossing down a glass of whiskey, he turned to me, saying, "My God, Joan, where did you get that damned black dress?" Between liquor and his poor eyesight, he sometimes confused me with Joan, who had not yet changed her dark hair to blond. (Mine was black.) He had returned to his room when Constance, dressed in a perfectly tailored suit of navy blue, flew across the living room and out the front door, leaving behind the perfume of gardenias and a dirty look cast in my direction. (Among the Hollywood detestables, even I was no match for Constance, who could sit across from me at the dinner table in Marion Davies' beach house and never acknowledge my existence with so much as an icy nod.) Barbara finally appeared, wearing Constance's beige gabardine suit. We lunched on chocolate milkshakes at a drugstore, after which she took me to the smart hairdressing shop of Saveli, where Saveli himself attended to my hair. He shortened my bangs to a line above my eyebrows, shaped the sides in points at my cheekbones, and shingled the back of my head. Barbara was pleased. "As a mat-tra-fact, Pie Face," she said, "you are beginning to look almost human."

It was then that Barbara introduced me to a group of Wall Street men who made it possible for me to buy expensive clothes. These most eligible bachelors in their thirties, finding débutantes a threat, turned to pretty girls in the theatre, whose mothers weren't husband-hunting. Café society developed about this time. The theatre, Hollywood, and society mingled in the monthly Mayfair dances at the Ritz, where society women could monitor their theatrical enemies and snub them publicly. All the rich men were friends who entertained one another in their perfectly appointed Park Avenue apartments and Long Island homes. The extravagant sums given to the girls for clothes were part of the fun—part of competing to see whose girl would win the Best-Dressed title. Sexual submission was not a condition of this arrangement, although many affairs grew out of it. For a time, Barbara was kept by William Rhinelander Stewart, who gave her a square-cut emerald from Cartier. One night, when we were swimming off Caleb Bragg's houseboat, the *Masquerader*, she watched it slip off her finger into Long Island Sound. She kept this hilarious accident secret from Stewart by buying a fake-emerald ring from Denis Smith, whose jewelry business was unknown to innocent lovers. They would have been staggered to learn how many of their gifts were converted into imitations and cash. Truly, ours was a heartless racket. After receiving an ermine coat from Jaeckel's, the gift of a stockbroker named John Lock, I let him take me just once to a tea dance at the Biltmore Hotel.

In 1924, shopping on my own proved fatal. I would buy anything a persuasive salesgirl thrust upon me. A childish short pink dress was responsible for getting me thrown out of the Algonquin Hotel. In May, when the Denishawn tour ended, Barbara stuffed me into that hotel because, she said, "you will meet influential people at the Algonquin, and you don't want to spend the rest of your life on tour, washing and pressing costumes." I didn't give a damn about influential people, and I hated my dark little room, with its old-fashioned brass bedstead. The owner of the Algonquin was Frank Case, a tall, thin middle-aged man, who spent much of his time in the lobby among his guests. One afternoon, as I stepped out of the elevator, I found him waiting for me.

"How old are you, Miss Brooks?" Mr. Case asked.

"Seventeen," I said.

"Are you sure you aren't fourteen?"

"Yes."

"Does your family know you are here?"

"Yes."

"Well," said Mr. Case, walking me away from the elevator, "George Cohan just phoned to tell me that last night he came down in the elevator with a fourteen-year-old black-haired girl in a little pink dress. Where were you going at two o'clock in the morning?"

"To meet Barbara Bennett at Texas Guinan's—the El Fay Club."

"Well," said Mr. Case again, frowning down at me, "you are creating a scandal in the hotel which must stop. I have arranged for you to move to the Martha Washington, a respectable women's hotel on East Twenty-ninth Street, where you will be much better off. When can you move?"

"Right now," I said.

I felt disgusted with myself as I packed my trunk. This humiliating eviction could not have taken place if I'd been wearing a fashionable slinky dress and a hat.

The atmosphere of the Martha Washington Hotel was institutional. The women wore short hair, suits, and sensible shoes, and worked, I assumed, in offices. Two weeks after I had been assigned a cell under the roof, I went into the grim, nearly empty dining room for tea. To my amazement, sitting alone at a large table was the exotic star of the film *Java Head*, Jetta Goudal. While I ate a ham sandwich and drank iced tea, I watched her welcome to her table a group of girls, some of them bringing gifts. She was particularly pleased with a handmade shawl of white wool, which she threw over her shoulders.

"Does Jetta Goudal *live* here?" I asked my waitress.

"Yes, Miss."

"Is this her birthday?"

"No, Miss, this happens once a month. Those girls are her fans."

Before I could investigate Jetta Goudal's tea parties any further, I was asked to leave the Martha Washington, because people in a building over-looking the hotel had been shocked to see me on the roof, exercising in "flimsy pajamas." Within a month, my wearing apparel had got me kicked out of two hotels. On my own this time, I moved to the Wentworth, an unpre-tentious theatrical hotel on West Forty-sixth Street.

My dress problem had become acute. I couldn't trust ordinary salesgirls, and the clothes that suited the slim, long-legged Bennetts looked dreadful on my short, dancer's body. One night, I saw in a theatre program a photograph of Marilyn Miller, the Ziegfeld star, posed in a stunning evening gown from Milgrim, a fashionable store then on Broadway at Seventy-fourth Street. The next morning, I took five hundred dollars in cash to Milgrim's and handed it to Miss Rita, a salesgirl from the Bronx, who had never before been exposed to such a straightforward confession of ignorance in dress. Neither she nor I could guess that in 1926 my photograph would advertise Milgrim in theatre programs, but she did sense an extraordinary intensity in one who appeared to be a chorus girl with a windfall. She studied my face, my figure, my move-ments closely, while I looked at the models showing evening clothes. After I had seen them all, she selected for me an evening gown of white crystal bugle beads, and a silver cloth evening coat with a white fox collar. When I came for my first fitting, I met an exuberant Italian woman, who, because I had small, firm breasts, slashed my evening gowns almost to the navel. My back she left bare. Sitting at a restaurant or nightclub table, I was a nearly naked sight to behold. Miss Rita chose my afternoon dresses in pastel shades of satin and silk crêpes. My suits were severely tailored by Gus, who stuck pins in me when I didn't stand still. At last, my beloved New York was able to present a Louise Brooks who was neither Kansas nor Broadway nor Hollywood nor Park Avenue but uniquely herself. Late in 1924, I became a chorus girl in *George White's Scandals*, and the next year a specialty dancer in the *Ziegfeld Follies*.

By 1925, I was living at the Marguery, an apartment hotel on Park Avenue at Forty-seventh Street, in a large room that looked down on three fine spruce trees crooning peacefully in the courtyard. That same John Lock who had given me the ermine coat had also given me a riding outfit and a course of riding lessons at Durland's Riding Academy, on Seventy-ninth Street. My riding master, Hugo, had been the groom of a German cavalry officer. He was small and compact, made for a commanding seat on a horse. My seat was so bad that he considered it a miracle every time the quiet little mare named Beauty carried me safely across Central Park West onto the bridle path in Central Park. On a mild morning in December, as we turned uptown on the bridle path, I presented to Hugo my weekly gift of a pint of brandy. Next to being separated from horses, his greatest fear was that of being separated from liquor in our land of Prohibition and thus finding himself hideously sober. For some horsy reason, Beauty, on that occasion, used our customary brandy ceremony as an excuse to run away. Instead of racing to save me, Hugo trotted behind, laughing his head off, and left my rescue to two mounted policemen, who galloped up on either side of me, snatched the reins from my hands, and brought Beauty to a halt.

Later that morning, while a woman named Mrs. Gard gave me my weekly massage, I laughed with her about my poor horsemanship and Hugo's unchivalrous conduct. She was one of the few people who loved me. And, oddly, I loved her, too. I loved her corpulent figure, in its tight black coat, and her kind, red Irish face under the old-fashioned hat decorated with a bird wing. I loved the tenderness with which she "cracked" my neck, almost snapping my head off, and her concern with my too-short shoes, which were "growing horns" on my heels. I could never get her to gossip about her famous clients—for instance, Mrs. William Randolph Hearst, whose husband was living openly with the movie star Marion Davies. But then neither did Mrs. Gard express her sorrow for my careless disposal of the body over which she sweated, contributing to its seductiveness. Nevertheless, I could hear it in her voice as she asked about a new beaver coat flung in a chair. "Oh, that," I said. "Walter

Wanger sent it to me." A good Catholic, she knew that Walter was a married man. At that time, I was portraying a bathing beauty in *The American Venus*, a film that was being shot at Famous Players-Lasky's Long Island studio in Astoria, and Wanger was an executive in the Famous Players-Lasky (later to become Paramount) New York office, where I had recently signed a five-year contract.

One day, Mrs. Gard had just left me smelling of camphor oil and sitting in bed in a woolly bathrobe when the phone rang announcing the arrival of Ruth Waterbury, a staff writer on the magazine *Photoplay*. The publicity department of the Paramount New York office gave me no guidance in dealing with the press. I got along well enough with the New York journalists I knew as a chorus girl. But I could see I was in trouble the moment Ruth Waterbury, from Hollywood, entered my room, because she looked greatly surprised and greatly displeased to find me in bed. She had obviously expected me to take her to lunch at the chic Marguery Restaurant. I couldn't ask her to wait while I bathed and dressed, so I asked whether she would like lunch served in my room. She said something about not being hungry, pulled a chair close to the bed, sat down, and removed a pad and pencil from her handbag. Possessing that precious quality of youth—indifference to the censure of those whom one did not admire—I found my composure equal to an hour of Miss Waterbury's hostility. Her method of interviewing me was to recount the publicity office's story of my "sudden success," expecting to be able to write that I responded with rapture about going to Hollywood. Her notetaking stopped when she discovered that I was not overwhelmed by the magic of Hollywood, and that I hadn't wanted to leave Ziegfeld but had let the screenwriter Townsend Martin persuade me to play a part in his film *The American Venus*. Whereas she looked upon me as a stupid "chorus girl" who didn't appreciate her astonishing good luck, I looked upon her as artistically retarded not to know that ten years of professional dancing was the best possible preparation for "moving" pictures. She told me how wonderful it was to go from a small part in *The American Venus* to the lead opposite the great star Adolphe Menjou in *A Social Celebrity*, directed by the boy genius of high comedy Malcolm St. Clair. I asked her if she had ever seen Ruth St. Denis and Ted Shawn dance, or if she had heard of Martha Graham's sensational success in the *Greenwich Village Follies*. She had not. I didn't realize then that this small cultural conflict with Ruth Waterbury was merely the first instance of the kind of contempt that was destined to drive me out of Hollywood.

TWO | *On Location with Billy Wellman*

Early in the autumn of 1925, when I was eighteen, two film companies, Metro-Goldwyn-Mayer and Paramount, each offered me a five-year contract. Not knowing what to do about either contract, which would separate me from my dream of becoming a great dancer, I went to my best friend, Walter Wanger, for advice. How sweet he was then: a brilliant, laughing young man of the world whose heart remained very tender. He had taken me under his protection after meeting me while I was a specialty dancer in the *Ziegfeld Follies* and after discovering that my blasé insolence was a masquerade. It amused him to find that the decadent black-and-white Aubrey Beardsley makeup covered a sprinkling of Kansas freckles. It aroused his sympathy to learn that my bold décolletage of glittering white sequins was actually an attempt to conceal my childish insecurity. If, at this crucial moment in my career, Wanger had given me some faith in my screen personality and my acting ability, he might have saved me from the predators who prowled Broadway and Hollywood. Instead, failing to understand that I put no value on my beauty and sexual attractiveness and could not use them as a means to success, he advised me as if my career depended on nothing else.

It was while I was having supper in Wanger's apartment that I told him about the two film offers. I was so sure he would advise me to sign the Paramount contract that the emotional impact of his unexpected response has kept the scene vivid in my memory. I can still feel the pride I took in my new black velvet suit and emerald cuff links, still smell the russet chrysanthemums in their crystal vase on the table, still see the glowing reds and purples of the fruit compote set in a silver bowl of ice. The compote I never tasted.

Just as I picked up my spoon, Walter said, "You must sign the contract with M-G-M." I sat back in my chair, speechless, and then began to cry. "Don't you see that your friendship with me would put you in a dangerously vulnerable position at Paramount?" he said. "Everybody would assume that you owed your contract to me, and all the producers would treat you accordingly. If you sign with M-G-M, you will start fresh—completely independent, on your own."

But I did not see. "You just say that because you don't want me at Paramount," I said, sobbing. "And you think I am a bad actress."

Laughing, he protested, "No, no, no. It's because you can't take care of yourself. The fact is you ought to get married."

"Get married!" I said, bursting into fresh mascara-blackened tears. "There, you see?—you don't even like me."

My total misconstruction of Walter's advice and warning made it inevitable that I would sign the Paramount contract. And for a time he proved a false prophet. I was always welcome in his office, where my studio problems were solved with more gaiety than serious consideration. In July, 1926, when I did get married, to the director Edward Sutherland, Walter blessed the occasion with a sterling-silver cocktail set from Cartier. In 1927, he convinced me that I need not feel lost and afraid when the Astoria studio was closed and I was sent from its intimate friendliness to the factory coldness of the Hollywood studio. But then, in the early part of 1928, Walter left Paramount, and I had no sympathetic studio contact whatever. The head of production was B. P. Schulberg, whom I did not know. He had been catapulted into this position because he had Clara Bow under personal contract. In 1927, after the release of *Mantrap* and *It*, Clara had become Hollywood's top female box-office star.

In April, 1928, I divorced Eddie Sutherland—leaving a pretty house in Laurel Canyon, where we had done a lot of entertaining, for a lonely suite in the Beverly Wilshire Hotel. Staring down at my name in lights on the marquee of the Wilshire Theatre was like reading an advertisement of my isolation. Someday, I thought, I would run away from Hollywood forever. Not just the temporary running away I did after making each of my films—but forever.

In May, when the studio wanted me in order to start production on *Beggars of Life*, under the direction of William Wellman, it had to track me from Hollywood to New York and on to Miami, then to Havana, to Palm Beach, and, finally, to Washington, where I was visiting George Marshall, the owner of the professional football team the Redskins. While waiting for the capture of a seemingly reluctant actress he had never met, Billy Wellman came to the unfortunate conclusion that since I did not follow the pattern of the actors who haunted the studio panting after film roles, I did not care about making films at all. Because he did not know that sycophancy had no merit in the New York studio where I had begun my career, and because I was unaware that prudent Hollywood actors wooed producers, directors, and writers with flattering attention, a coldness was set up between us which neither of us could dispel. Nor did hard work on my part and a willingness to do dangerous stunts under his direction alter Billy's conclusion. In 1932, at the bar of Tony's Restaurant in New York, he asked, "Why did you always hate making pictures, Louise?" Those were the last words I ever heard him speak. Before that, this intricate man had offered me a part in *The Public Enemy*, then passed it on to Jean Harlow when I turned it down in order to make a trip to New York.

Bewitched by his own success in Hollywood, he could not imagine my hating the place.

It was not surprising that when we met for the first time, on the set where I was to make a test with Richard Arlen for *Beggars of Life*, Billy greeted me with more suspicion than cordiality. For my part, I was suspicious about making the test. I had been required to make a test for no previous film. Billy explained that Benjamin Glazer, who had written the screenplay and was supervising the film, thought my forehead was "too high" to photograph well without my bangs, which were unsuitable for one aspect of my role—my disguise as a boy. To test my naked brow, Billy chose a scene from the film in which Dick and I spend a chaste night together in the hollow of a haystack.

During the twenties, no director was considered any good who could not make his actors cry real tears, and no actor was considered any good who could not shed real tears on demand. Tears without facial contortions! Luckily, I had acquired this art from my mother, whose soft hazel eyes could overflow at any suggestion of sadness, from the smell of burning beans to a Wagner *Leitmotiv*. However, Billy wasn't only interested in my tears in the scene. He wanted Dick to cry, too, and Dick was not a spontaneous weeper. He had come on the set with his tramp clothes lovingly dirtied and an enthusiastic three days' growth of beard, but he couldn't squeeze out a single tear before the camera. While the hot lights converted the hollow of the haystack into an oven, Billy shot the scene again and again, determined to make Dick cry if it took all day—and it did. Sometime after six, he resorted to the fiction that Dick's mother was dying. Richard wept. Thankfully, Billy directed the scene so well that it went into the picture without a retake, and my "too-high" forehead was forgotten.

The first ten days of production were spent at the studio, shooting the interior of a farmhouse. I play the adopted daughter of a repulsive old farmer who, as I serve him breakfast on a summer morning, tries to rape me. Breaking out of his grasp, I grab a shotgun and kill him. As I prepare to run away, disguised as a boy, a young tramp (Richard Arlen) appears at the screen door looking for a handout. After I explain the circumstances of the farmer's death, Dick decides to befriend me, and together we begin the flight from billposters carrying my photograph and the notice WANTED FOR MURDER. Billy directed this opening sequence of *Beggars of Life* with a sure, dramatic swiftness that the rest of the film lacked. The early pace did not accord with Glazer's artistic conception of the tragedy, and thereafter the action grew slower while contributing nothing more to the film's content. Only Wallace Beery's entrance into the film, as Oklahoma Red, an older tramp, saved it from the consequences of Glazer's cultured supervision. Neither God nor the Devil could have influenced Beery's least gesture before the camera. Having been a tramp briefly as a boy, he developed his character with authority and variety. His Oklahoma Red is a little masterpiece.

On the last day of May, Wally drove me to Jacumba, California, high in the Jacumba Mountains, near the Mexican border, where we were to shoot sixteen days of the film's thirty-nine-day schedule. Always, I had been scared stiff when anyone drove faster than forty miles an hour. But as I sat beside that bear with his open black Packard racing up the treacherous mountain curves, I enjoyed one of the most exhilarating experiences of my life. Wally drove with perfect ease, as if he and the Packard constituted a single unit of control and power. When, to avoid hitting a dog, he skidded off the road for an instant, my composure amazed me.

"You must be the best driver in the whole world," I said.

"Not only the best but the safest," he said.

Sure now that Wally was a man of courage, I said, "Some directors call you a coward."

Unperturbed, he said, "That's because I won't do the stunts and fight scenes that my double is hired to do. Have you got a double for location?"

I said I had.

"Then don't let that crazy Wellman talk you into doing any stunts yourself because he says it will make the picture better. That's a lot of bunk. Nobody seeing the picture will know the difference, while you are liable to be dead or in a wheelchair."

It was six o'clock and boiling hot when we stopped in front of the Jacumba Hotel, which was a blistered gray two-story building with a sagging porch. Wally gave a grunt of disgust as we entered the shabby lobby. With Anna, my Russian maid, who had just arrived by train with my trunks, I went to inspect a primitive bedroom and bath on the ground floor which had been assigned me. When I returned to the lobby, Wally was talking to a man about Jacumba's auxiliary airfield. In 1927, when I was in a comedy with Wally called *Now We're in the Air*, he had learned to fly and had bought a plane. Now, deciding that he could never endure two weeks in the Jacumba Hotel, he arranged to fly up from Hollywood for each day's work. As I sat on the sagging porch watching him and the Packard speed away, I felt like one abandoned. The owner of the hotel, a Mr. Vaughan, said it would be some time before the rest of the company, presumably driving at less magical speeds, could be expected to arrive.

Mr. Vaughan also owned the entire town, an expanse of three hundred acres, and provided employment for its inhabitants—all four hundred of them. He had built Jacumba in 1919 as a summer resort where the farmers of the Imperial Valley might escape from the desert heat and bathe in the local mineral springs. Situated on the railroad running between San Diego and Yuma, it was an ideal location for *Beggars of Life*, because there were only four trains a day, leaving many hours free for our private freight train to run back and forth before the camera. Photographically, the track, spinning down the mountains among deep canyons, was superb.

About eight o'clock, Billy Wellman, with his wife and Dick Arlen, arrived in a company car. The crew and a caravan of trucks arrived about nine o'clock. A bus carrying the remaining members of the cast unloaded about ten o'clock. They were twenty riotous hoboes selected by Billy from among the outcasts who financed leisurely drunks by working as extras in films. The inhabitants of Jacumba watched them with somber disapproval as they plowed into the pool hall next to the hotel. (Its proprietor, Carlos, was also the town bootlegger.) In spite of the money to be made out of "those picture people," the local people strongly resented our taking charge of their town. The arrival of the hoboes not only intensified their resentment, it spread the spirit of conflict among the members of the company. To throw together a group of people with incompatible social backgrounds in that tiny, remote community was an invitation to mischief. By the time our work on location was finished, only our private freight train remained an object of admiration and respect.

We fell in love with Locomotive 102 on the first morning, when she gave two long and two short blasts on her steam whistle to call us to work from breakfast in the lunchroom. Indulgent, she let us ride all over the train—astride the cow catcher, in the engine cab, atop boxcars, inside gondolas, and on flatcars. I chose to ride in the caboose, with its cozy bunks and fat little black stove, which glowed red in the cold mountain nights. When everyone was accounted for by the assistant director, and after a warning ring of her bell, away Locomotive 102 skipped—up the canyons on the hour's trip to Carrizo Gorge, the central point from which we operated. If work finished at sunset, she returned to town in a frolicking mood, with clanging bell and blasting whistle. If work finished at night, she coasted to town on the breeze, with all of us lying out on the flatcars, looking up at the stars shimmering in the black sky. Number 102 was a locomotive to make her engineer, her fireman, and her brakeman proud. Under Billy's expert guidance, she learned numerous tricks of changing speed and direction, of starting and stopping, with perfect timing. The difficulty of the train crew's work taught its members to respect ours, which was hard and dangerous and, to them, often foolhardy. They were dazed by the unconcern with which a runaway flatcar and the caboose were plunged into the gorge, taking with them the second camera and missing the second cameraman by inches. They were dismayed when Billy persuaded me to take the place of my double, Harvey, and hop a fast-moving boxcar, which nearly sucked me under its wheels.

So fascinated was I by a quiet sadism practiced by Billy behind the camera, especially in his direction of women, that I began to investigate his past life. From him I learned nothing, because he was extremely shy in conversation with women. A slim, handsome young man, he resembled an actor who was uncertain in his part more than he did a director. It was from Richard Arlen, who had recently worked many months with Billy on *Wings*, that I obtained Billy's history. Having finished with our particular scenes early one night, Billy sent Dick and me back to town in the cab of Number 102. While I was getting my mail at the hotel desk, Dick surprised me by darting over to the pool hall, returning with a bottle of whiskey, and asking me to have a drink. I was surprised partly because Dick was the undefiled type who did not touch booze and also because his winning smile concealed a strong dislike for me, which was not fully explained, I thought, by the fact that when we worked together in 1927 on a film entitled *Rolled Stockings* his vanity had made him quickly aware that I did not admire his acting. With a motive of my own added to my curiosity about his motive, I sat down with him on a greasy brown leather couch in the lobby. The night clerk set a pitcher of ice water and two glasses on an old piano bench that served as a coffee table. Dick poured two powerful drinks and began a worshipful account of Billy's career which went as follows:

In 1917, like many other untried heroes of nineteen, Billy was captivated by the glorious publicity given the Lafayette Escadrille, the squadron of American pilots fighting with the French in the First World War. Those highly colored tales of superheroes, calculated to help bring the United States into the war, led Billy to join a French ambulance corps, which, not requiring him to swear allegiance to France, did not require him to forfeit his American citizenship. After transferring to the French flying corps and shooting down "some" German planes, he returned to the United States in 1918 to instruct cadets at Rockwell Field, in San Diego. His Croix de Guerre and the fame of the Lafayette Escadrille, which made him a hero in Hollywood, were the foundation upon which he built his career. From an actor he became an assistant director, then a director of Westerns, and in 1926 he was selected to direct the First World War film *Wings*. Its spectacular success established him as a top director and coupled his name forever with the Lafayette Escadrille.

In September, 1927, the magazine *Motion Picture* published an article about *Wings*, called "Warriors of the Sky," stating that the director, "William Wellman, a former member of the Lafayette Escadrille, had been wounded and decorated in the war." By the time an interview with Wellman by Ezra Goodman, "Roman Candle of M-G-M," appeared in the March, 1953, issue of *Esquire*, Billy's experiences with the Lafayette Escadrille had become escapades of surpassing wonder. Then, in 1964, Random House published *The Lafayette Escadrille*, by Herbert Molloy Mason, Jr. Nowhere in the text does the name of William A. Wellman appear, and Mason comments on the fact that "by 1931 more than 4,000 men laid false claim to having shared in the Lafayette Escadrille's glory." In the back of his book, Mason lists American pilots who flew with French operational escadrilles other than the Lafayette. In this list appears the name of Sgt. William Wellman, who served with the Escadrille Spad 87 and shot down two German planes. Billy ended his career in 1958 with the direction of a film he himself wrote—*Lafayette Escadrille*. Two years after the publication of Mason's book, an interview with Wellman appeared in the July, 1966, issue of the Beverly Hills magazine *Cinema*. On being asked about the film *Lafayette Escadrille*, Billy said it had nothing to do with the the Lafayette Escadrille. When he was asked whether he was in the fabulous Lafayette Escadrille, he said, "I was a member of the Lafayette Flying Corps."

But even as Dick related the Wellman history in 1928 I did not quite believe it. My heroes did not advocate the abuse of women. My heroes were men of action who pursued death as unyieldingly as did Tommy Hitchcock, the hero of Billy's own Squad 87. (Hitchcock was to die at last, in 1939, as the result of a fall on the polo field.) Sensing my lack of enthusiasm, Dick attempted to strengthen his position as an authority on flying heroes by adding that he himself had flown with the Royal Air Force in the First World War. I laughed at him. "Really, Dick," I said, "it's hard for me to believe that you, an American boy born in 1900, could have flown with the RAF in a war that ended in November, 1918."

Combined with the unaccustomed doses of bootleg whiskey, this remark was all that was needed to release what was unmistakably a prepared assault. Dick's jaw muscles twitched, as he hunched closer to me to deliver his mono-logue. "It sure is too bad about your getting a divorce from a swell guy like Eddie Sutherland—and a swell director," he said. "Now that you're not his wife anymore, everybody expects Paramount to fire you. They don't know you're a pet of the front office." He paused for a philosophic sigh. "Funny thing. I've been working at Paramount for three years—a damned fine actor, too—and I make a stinking four hundred dollars a week, while you ride around in your damn Lincoln town car with its damn 'black satin' finish. *You*— why, you can't even act! You're not even good-looking. You're a lousy actress and your eyes are too close together." Having concluded his curse upon me and my Lincoln town car, Dick stood up, snatched away his bottle of whiskey, and swaggered from the lobby.

The following morning, Dick and I did not work. When we met at the huge cement swimming pool round which the town was built, his nice-guy grin was back in place and nothing was said about the incident of the night before. To confirm his self-approval, he gave a diving exhibition from the spring-board while Jack Chapin and I sat on a bench and watched. Jack was the seventeen-year-old brother of Billy Wellman's wife, Marjery, who was also our script girl. Like her, Jack was a tall, pretty redhead. Engaged as a hobo extra on the film, he had attached himself to me as a sort of page and de-cided not to work when I did not work. The hoboes openly condemned him for taking advantage of his relationship to Wellman, as did my double, Harvey, who joined us at the pool while Dick was performing. Estimating Dick's skill at a glance, Harvey climbed to the top of the thirty-foot tower and began a series of dives that retired Dick to our bench and left me enchanted. The vulgar face and mind I knew him to possess formed no part of this Harvey, executing aerial turns and twists comparable in grace to that of some capricious bird in flight. When Harvey was satisfied with his triumph over Dick, he joined us for a Coca-Cola. "How come you aren't out on location with the rest of the hoboes?" he asked Jack.

Jack said he was *not* a hobo, and, besides, he had hurt his back.

"Yeah?" Harvey sneered, punching him between the shoulders. "It looks OK to me."

That night, we worked in the hobo "jungle," a deep pit in Carrizo Gorge. In its center, a rock fireplace had been built, before which we gathered when we were not needed for a scene. A hobo known as Tiny, who weighed four hundred pounds, occupied a rock seat that had been built for him beside the fireplace. Because he moved with great difficulty, Billy had thoughtfully appointed him keeper of the fire and brewer of the coffee kept steaming in an enormous graniteware pot on a grill set over the fire. As a sideline, Tiny collected and disseminated all the company gossip. While Jack and I were listening to a tale of how the hoboes had become enraged by the rise in the price of liquor at the pool hall and had badly beaten Carlos with his own pool cues, someone yelled, "Jack! Jack!" from the top of the pit, where Billy was shooting a scene with Wally Beery. Thinking that Billy wanted him, Jack scrambled up the steep incline and disappeared in the glare of the arc lamps just as the actor Robert Perry joined us before the fire. Ordinarily unmoved by anything (including his own fine performance in *Beggars of Life*), he was childishly happy now as he produced a quart of Scotch from his coat pocket, outsmarting Prohibition.

"I sneaked this across the border from Mexicali," Perry said. "That thief Carlos' closing the pool hall can't keep me from drinking." Then, with a sly smile, he added, "I saw a beautiful picture of you there, too."

"Oh, where?" I asked.

"In one of the cribs, over this Mexican girl's bed," he said. "She's a big fan of yours."

The sound of something crashing through scrub oak amid falling rocks turned our attention to the steep incline. We saw Jack stumble to his feet on the canyon floor while voices jeered from the top, "How's your back now, Jackie boy?"

A few minutes later, Billy and Wally came down to the fire for coffee. Billy was amused by Jack, who was near tears, mumbling, "They tripped me, the dirty rats. They tripped me." Wally was disgusted with the trick. He loathed the gags that added needless hazards to filming on location. Besides, the distraction of the noisy trick had ruined his last scene. Away from work a honey bear, Beery was the meanest bear alive on the set; and now, when he growled that he hated working at night, that it was cold, and that the box lunches were rotten, Billy immediately called the night's work finished. Much wiser than directors who tried to dominate Wally, Billy let him play his scenes as he liked and, as often as possible, let him work when he liked.

To shoot the most dangerous and difficult stunt in the picture, Billy waited until the engineer and Locomotive 102 had become professional in their response to direction. In this scene, the brakeman, discovering Dick and me hiding in a gondola, forces us to climb outside onto the iron ladder and jump from the speeding freight train. Dick's double had a comparatively easy fall, because he jumped of his own accord to a spot a short distance below the track. My double, Harvey, was asked by Billy to make a thrilling plunge deep into the canyon, made more dangerous because Harvey must appear to fall after the brakeman had brought down his club on his hands clinging to the ladder. A hundred-foot dive into water was a routine stunt for Harvey. A twenty-five-foot dive into a rocky canyon was another matter. He agreed to do it on condition that he do the stunt just once. No rehearsals. No retakes. Just once. In preparation, Number 102 and Billy and Harvey cruised up and down the track to find the right spot for the fall. Then Harvey, with the company crew, cleared the rocks and scrub oak from his path down the incline and dug up a soft bed of soil at the spot where he intended to land. After that, the cars were hooked on to Number 102 and Henry Gerrard, our cameraman, mounted his camera on top of the boxcar next to the gondola. Then the train went forward and back until the speed of the train and the moment and the spot of the fall were synchronized. Number 102 was to give a sharp toot as she passed the spot, and Billy was to count so many seconds and yell "Go!" With that, Harvey would take the plunge. First, a shot of me clinging to the ladder was filmed to make sure my background would match the background of Harvey's fall. Then he took his place on the ladder. Number 102 backed up again and started forward, gaining speed rapidly until the whistle tooted, Billy counted the seconds and yelled "Go!," and Harvey fell away down the gorge. Nobody spoke while the train returned to the spot and we saw Harvey sprawled motionless upon the incline. Nobody spoke after the train stopped until Billy cried, "My God, I've killed him!" At that, Harvey, pleased with his joke, got up, laughing, and waved his arms to indicate no broken bones. With his safe return to the gondola, all of us except Billy, who had taken the pledge for the duration of production, celebrated the success of the single shot with toasts drunk to Harvey's skill and courage, to Billy for his mastery of stunt direction, to Henry Gerrard and his camera, which had followed every inch of the fall, and to the engineer and our darling Number 102.

On the trip home that night, I lay out on a flatcar between Jack and Harvey. As the bell clanged the approach of town, I turned to Harvey, whispering, "At one o'clock, come round to my bedroom window. I'll open the screen and let you in."

The next morning, Billy worked alone with the freight train. Harvey and some of the hoboes were lounging on the hotel porch as I crossed it to return to my room after breakfast. "Just a minute, Miss Brooks," Harvey said in a loud voice as he rose from the porch rail and sauntered over to me. "I've got something to ask you." Holding the door shut with one hand while his other hand held my arm, he said, "I guess you know my job depends on my health." Naming a high film executive whom I had never met, he went on, "Everybody knows you're his girl and he has syphilis, and what I want to know is, Do you have syphilis?" Following an impressive moment of silence, he ended by saying, "Another reason I want to know is that my girl is coming up at noon to drive me back to Hollywood." Looking round to get the effect of his performance upon the hoboes, Harvey saw Robert Perry moving quietly toward him. Quickly dropping his hands, Harvey sauntered off the porch as I opened the door and fled to my room.

At one o'clock, praying that everyone had eaten and gone, I went to the lunchroom. It was empty except for two people sitting at the counter—Harvey and his girl. She was a fat slattern in a yellow housedress. Harvey nudged her, and she swung round on her stool to stare at me and giggle while he spoke to her in an undertone. Just as I finished my ice cream and was preparing to make my escape, Billy came in from location and sat down at my table for lunch. When Harvey came to say goodbye to him, it was obvious that Billy had heard every detail of our sordid affair—from the entrance through my bedroom window to the denouement on the hotel porch. He could not resist a small leer in my direction. How the grand Louise Brooks had fallen! It was a sequence he could have directed with relish.

On the last day of location, I was snoozing in a bunk in the caboose when a burning sensation on my thigh awakened me and I found a lighted cigarette in my pants pocket. Next to lighting newspaper fires under people sitting in canvas chairs, this was the favorite company gag. As I sat up to pull the cigarette out, saying, "Who the hell did this?," the front door of the caboose closed on the prankster, and the back door opened to admit Robert Perry. During the filming of *Beggars of Life*, we had become good friends, and now he had come to say goodbye. That reminded me of Jack, and I said I hadn't seen him all day.

Robert said, "Your boyfriend had a little accident—"

"*My* boyfriend?" I interrupted.

"That's what he thinks he is," Robert said, giving me a curious look. But I was too eager to hear about Jack's accident to pause over such a ridiculous notion. The day before, Robert told me, Jack was cavorting over the locomotive near the whistle when someone blew it, giving him a nasty steam burn on his bare back. That afternoon, he had been sent to Hollywood in the car with the boys who were taking the rushes—the day's work—to the laboratory.

One evening a month later, the telephone operator in the Beverly Wilshire Hotel rang my suite to announce that Jack Chapin was in the lobby. I told her to send him up. He entered my sitting room, looking strange and formal, dressed in a blue coat and white pants, his red curls slicked down with some strongly scented oil. He did not talk; he did not drink the Bacardi cocktail I mixed for him. He sat on one sofa before the fireplace, staring at me sitting on the opposite sofa, and then, without warning, leaped at me and grappled me in his arms.

Too astonished to be angry, I shoved him away, saying, "Are you trying to make love to me?"

"Why not?" he said furiously, jumping up and backing away to the door to make his exit. "You go to bed with everyone else—why not me?"

THREE | *Marion Davies' Niece*

Nobody can know for certain why anyone commits suicide, but it seems likely that being Marion Davies' niece was one of the reasons for my friend Pepi Lederer's killing herself in 1935. And Marion's being the mistress of William Randolph Hearst was probably another. In 1929, and again in 1930, Pepi attempted to escape the effect of their overpowering celebrity and boundless wealth upon the subhumanity of Hollywood, which regarded her as nothing more than a sign pointing the way to Marion's beach house in Santa Monica; to Wyntoon, Mr. Hearst's estate in Northern California; to San Simeon, his castle overlooking the Pacific Ocean, halfway between Los Angeles and San Francisco; and to St. Donat's, his castle in Wales. In the summer of 1930, while Marion and Mr. Hearst, with their collection of guests, were traveling in Europe, Pepi persuaded them to let her remain in London, take a flat, and write for Mr. Hearst's deluxe quarterly *The Connoisseur*. To Marion and Mr. Hearst, whose idea of a great writer was the magazine writer Adela Rogers St. Johns, putting Pepi on *The Connoisseur*'s staff was only a way of disposing of her; they often disposed of people by giving them fake jobs on Hearst publications. In contrast to their serious treatment of her brother Charlie Lederer, for whom they obtained a screenwriting job at the Metro-Goldwyn-Mayer studio, their treatment of Pepi was that accorded a naughty, entertaining child, incapable of any serious endeavor.

Lacking the ability to perceive excellence, they did not realize that Pepi had the gift not only of seeing and paying attention but of doing so from a uniquely witty viewpoint—a combination that might have made her a great writer. But in all her twenty-five years (the last twelve of them spent with Marion) she had acquired no discipline of any sort. She could not discipline her gluttony, which, although she had a beautiful face and fine bone structure, made her fat and sexually unattractive, and she could not discipline her consumption of alcohol, which led to her addiction to cocaine, which, in turn, led to her death. And if she could not do this, then certainly she could not learn to write, for writing is perhaps the most disciplined of all the arts. In New York during the winter of 1930, before Marion and Mr. Hearst arrived in June to carry her off to Europe, she signed up for a course in writing at Columbia University. But she was so gratified by my laughter over her first paper, "Why I Wish to Become a Writer," that she decided she didn't need it. Pepi didn't return to the United States for five years. For the first three years, after she had rid herself of the job on *The Connoisseur*, her letters to me were jubilant. In London, she wrote, she was Pepi Lederer, a person in her own right, not a way station for would-be friends of Marion and Mr. Hearst. And, she informed me, she had found a lovely companion, Monica Morris, who had come to share her flat, her generous allowance, and Marion's charge accounts.

I had not trusted Pepi's taste in girlfriends since she took up with a scruffy little blond blues singer in 1929. In New York, running into Blyth Daly, the actress daughter of the noted actor Arnold Daly, and remembering that she had played in London in 1927, I asked her whether she knew a girl called Monica Morris, who had become an intimate friend of Pepi's. Blyth let out a howl: "My God, the Stage-Door Ferret! Don't tell me Monica has latched onto Pepi!" The facts were what I had feared. Blyth had given Monica the name of the Stage-Door Ferret because she was the most predatory among the mob of girls who had fought over Tallulah Bankhead when she became the darling of the London theatre in 1923. As Tallulah's pal, she inevitably met all the celebrities in London.

In 1934, during Pepi's fourth year in London, the tone of her letters became perceptibly subdued. Marion and Mr. Hearst and the guest collection were making their longest stay in Europe (from June through September) and she was cracking under the strain of devising plausible subterfuges for evading their company—the need for which I did not discover till she returned to New York. In residence or on tour, Marion and Mr. Hearst obliged their guests to be onstage whenever they shone forth; and Pepi, as their star entertainer, could not default without submitting to some painful scenes. At Pepi's behest, Marion had invited me on the 1930 trip to Europe. I had declined, because, as I told Pepi, I was sure to miss some performance and be caught in bed with a book and be shipped home. She understood. She told me that on the 1928 trip Sadie Murray, a hearty-Irish-type relative of Mrs. Hearst, had grown too boisterous and been shipped home from the Lido. It was a most humiliating experience.

Dario Borzani and I were appearing in a ballroom dance act at the Capitol Theatre, the week of April 12, 1935, when Pepi and Monica Morris arrived in New York from London. They would spend two weeks in a suite at Mr. Hearst's Ritz Tower Hotel, on Park Avenue, before going on to Hollywood and San Simeon. Monica had never before been in New York, but just about the first thing she said to me after we met was "Will you take me to Harlem to get some cocaine?" She was most urgent. On shipboard, she said, she had hidden her little white "packets" of "uppies" between the face towels in the bathroom of the stateroom, and the stewardess had carried them off with the soiled linen. I referred her to Tallulah Bankhead, at the Gotham Hotel, and Monica hurried out, leaving Pepi and me alone in the Ritz Tower for what was to be our last serious talk before her death.

As the door of the entrance hall closed behind Monica, Pepi and I stood looking at each other. She had beautiful blue eyes, and they were suddenly dark and attentive; they did not lie to me. Now I understood at least one of the things that had made her want to avoid Marion and Mr. Hearst—cocaine. To ease the tension, she laughed her old happy laugh and said as we walked into the living room, "Well, why don't you congratulate me? See how much weight I've lost?"

I did congratulate her. She was noticeably thinner, due to this same cocaine.

Opening a cabinet stocked with liquor, she said, "Do you want a drink?"

"No, thanks," I said. "I have to do the show at the Capitol, but you have one."

"Not just now," she said.

Had I needed anything to confirm my belief in her addiction, it would have been the sight of Pepi walking away empty-handed from two dozen bottles of booze. We sat down on a sofa, and she picked up a blue-and-white Lowestoft porcelain breakfast cup and saucer from the coffee table in front of us. Looking pleased, she said, "It's a present for Mr. Hearst." Then the new darkness shadowed her eyes again, and she added, "What a silly idea—giving Mr. Hearst a present." And then she began to talk about what had gone wrong the preceding summer, when Mr. Hearst and Marion were in Europe.

When, with Monica, she joined them in Spain, Pepi sensed something calculated, almost abusive behind Marion's usual warm hospitality and Mr. Hearst's usual generosity. Turning her attention to the guests, she also sensed something watchful, almost pleased behind their usual devotion. Mr. Hearst and Marion were still playing the gracious lord and his lady, and the guests were still responding with grateful expressions of joy, but the life had gone out of their performances. Although the fact was assumed to be unknown, *Operator 13*— just released—was Marion's last picture at M-G-M. Louis B. Mayer dared not renew her contract. The exhibitors were adamant. No amount of free Hearst publicity could fill their theatres when a Marion Davies picture was shown. In the fall, when she returned to Hollywood, she would be signing a contract to make four pictures at Warner Brothers. It was like leaving a palace for a stable. Even so, if these four pictures did not make money, Marion's career would be ended. All the Hollywood producers knew that Mr. Hearst was nearing bankruptcy and could no longer afford to produce her films. (When he finally relinquished financial control of his publications, in 1937, his debt amounted to $126 million.)

Pepi said that when Marion was drunk she discarded her modesty and cursed everyone who she felt had contributed to her ruined career. Given the chance, Marion said, she could have developed into a great dramatic actress. But from first to last W.R. had projected her as a doll-sweetheart out of the eighteen-nineties, in the manner of the D. W. Griffith heroines, who had come to be totally rejected in the nineteen-twenties. For this reason, M-G-M bestowed its most valuable properties upon Greta Garbo and Norma Shearer. It was the stigma of failure rather than the hope of success which was driving her to sign the Warner Brothers contract. She was to do as she pleased, W.R. said, because the end of her M-G-M contract had marked the end of his interest in her films. As for Mr. Hearst, Pepi told me, he privately said that the reason Louis B. Mayer was blocking his efforts to make Marion the biggest star in Hollywood was that Mayer was afraid that Hearst might usurp his production throne at M-G-M. The Jewish control of the film industry, Mr. Hearst thought, had worked against Marion's success. In September, 1934, he briefly broke away from his entourage in order to fly to Berlin for a much-publicized friendly call on Hitler, who approved of the isolationist policy of the Hearst newspapers. And now, Pepi continued, she dreaded returning to Hollywood, because she had heard that Marion's glory and Mr. Hearst's power were being cautiously undermined. Marion's first Warner Brothers picture, with the unfortunate title *Page Miss Glory*, looked like a failure in the rough cut, and Mr. Hearst was being secretly denounced as pro-Nazi.

I had not the heart to tell Pepi that Marion's and Mr. Hearst's supremacy in Hollywood was even more questionable than she envisioned. At M-G-M, Marion's "dressing-room" (actually a six-room hacienda) had been a symbol of rank. But as a result of its being expensively transported from there in three ad-vertised sections, to be reassembled on the Warner Brothers lot, it had become a six-room joke. Her young leading man, Dick Powell, had all Hollywood snick-ering about his affair with her. Mr. Hearst's situation was not so funny. Holly-wood Jews had been indignant over his visit to Hitler at a time when the Gestapo and the storm troopers were in full operation, when the free press and the film studios had been seized by decree, and when Jewish journalists and actors had been dismissed from their jobs and deprived of their German citizenship. But now the full import of his gesture was coming home to them.

Before Hitler, the American film industry had counted on Europe for its major profits, and on Germany for the cream of those profits. In 1933, Hitler's propaganda minister, Josef Goebbels, first banned certain American films because "they were held not to be conducive to fostering the right German view of life." By 1935, the German view of life had become so narrow that the American film industry knew that it was only a question of time before the industry would lose the whole of its German market. (With this in mind, Goebbels suggested to the American film companies in 1938 that they might sell their films freely in Germany if American theatres in key cities would show a number of Nazi propaganda films. Shortly after this suggestion, Leni Riefenstahl arrived in Hollywood with a print of her "documentary" film, *Olympia*, seeking, unsuccessfully, an American release for it.)

Pepi, under pressure from Monica, was returning to Hollywood at a time when the film executives were preoccupied with the doings of Hitler that would inevitably result in the loss of millions of dollars in profits. As a consequence of this preoccupation, M-G-M had given up the luxury of producing Marion Davies films. And, as a consequence of this action, Mr. Hearst and Marion were preoccupied with their loss of power and prestige. In an emotional crisis when only love and compassion could save Pepi's life, she was returning to a Hollywood where those qualities, always scarce, were now nonexistent.

When I departed Hollywood forever, in 1940, I thought that getting away from the place would automatically cure me of its pestiferous disease, playfully referred to there as "going Hollywood." I retired first to my father's home in Wichita, but there I found that the citizens could not decide whether they despised me for having once been a success away from home or for now being a failure in their midst. In 1943, I moved on to New York, where I found that the only well-paying career open to me, as an unsuccessful actress of thirty-six, was that of a call girl. I blacked out my past, refused to see my few remaining friends connected with movies, and began to flirt with fancies related to little bottles filled with yellow sleeping pills. Then, in 1956, James Card, the film curator at Eastman House, in Rochester, New York, persuaded me to move to Rochester, where I could study old films and write about bits

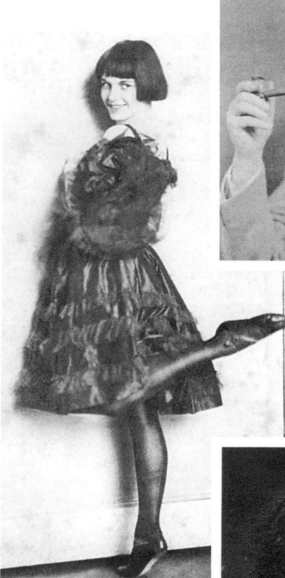

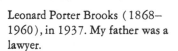

Leonard Porter Brooks (1868–1960), in 1937. My father was a lawyer.

Myra Rude Brooks (1884–1944), in 1903. My mother was an exquisite, self-taught pianist, who began her musical training on a church organ in the village of Burden, Kansas.

In Wichita, Kansas, 1921. I'm 15, wearing a dance costume.

In New York, a White Studio photo, 1923. I'm a Denishawn dancer.

In the ballet *The Feather of the Dawn*, with Ted Shawn, 1923.

My first film, a bit part in *Street of Forgotten Men*, 1925. Percy Marmont, the star, is at extreme right.

The American Venus, 1926. The photograph above was selected by Captain Joseph Medill Patterson, founder and eventually publisher of the New York *Daily News*, as the basis for the comic strip *Dixie Dugan* (1926–1954). The strip was written by J. P. McEvoy and drawn by J. H. Striebel.

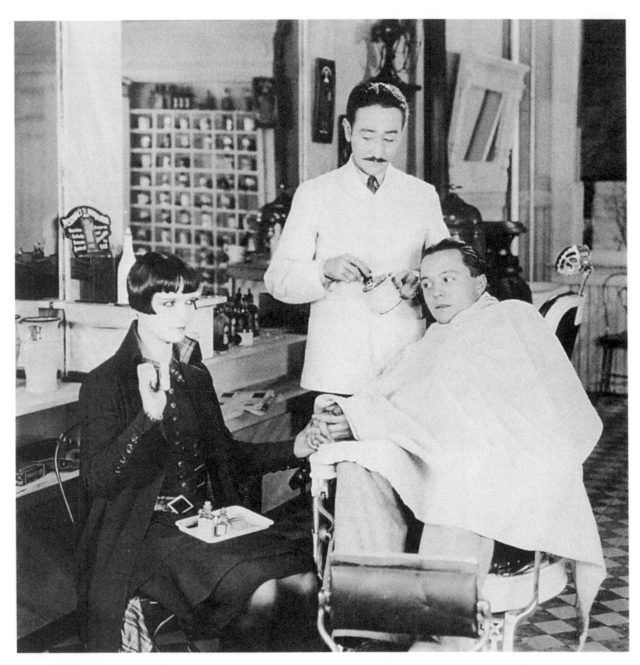

A publicity picture taken on the set of *A Social Celebrity*. The barber is Adolphe Menjou.

OPPOSITE. *A Social Celebrity*, 1926; (*below*) with Chester Conklin.

Love 'Em and Leave 'Em, 1926.

Just Another Blonde, 1926, with William Collier, Jr., and Dorothy Mackaill.

Rolled Stockings, 1927, with James Hall, *left,* and Richard Arlen.

Rolled Stockings; (*above*) with James Hall.

This is my favorite publicity still because I posed it
myself when I went to Hollywood in 1927. I found
myself looked upon as a literary wonder because I
read books. I'm posing with Keen Thompson, who
wrote the screenplay for *Now We're in the Air*.

OPPOSITE ABOVE. *Now We're in the Air*, 1927. I am speaking
to Raymond Hatton. Wallace Beery is at extreme right.

OPPOSITE BELOW. *The Show-off*, 1926, with Gregory Kelly.

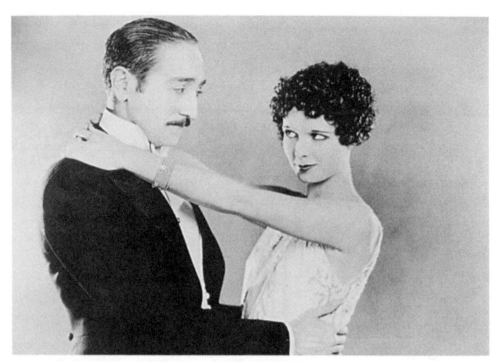

Evening Clothes, 1927: (*above*) with Adolph Menjou;
(*below*) with Menjou and Noah Beery.

ABOVE. On location for *Beggars of Life,* 1928. Richard Arlen, *left;* Billy Wellman has his head tied in a face towel; and Edgar Washington, *right.*
BELOW. With Jim Tully, who wrote the book *Outside Looking In,* from which *Beggars* was taken; Wallace Beery; and Richard Arlen.

With Richard Arlen in the boxcar scene in *Beggars of Life*.

of my rediscovered past. There I found that my recovery from the Hollywood disease had been wholly imaginary. I still judged all the films I had made while I was a movie actress not on their merits but by their success or failure in the eyes of Hollywood. I immediately set about correcting my vision.

By 1973, I was again positive of my cure, because I no longer accepted the Hollywood judgment that had condemned me to failure. As one liberated, I was studying the index of Fred Lawrence Guiles' biography *Marion Davies* when the name Pepi Lederer leaped up at me from a page and broke my heart. Never before in anything published about Marion had I seen Pepi's name. She had been dead for thirty-eight years, and now in my mind she suddenly came to life in a vivid series of sad and comic incidents, all supported by my almost perfect recollection of her words, as if I had unconsciously memorized a play in which she was the leading character. "Why have I never thought to write about Pepi?" I asked myself. And the answer came back to mock me: "Because she wasn't a success—she was a failure in Hollywood." I went to my bookshelves and pulled out an old dictionary, whose flyleaves were pasted with typewritten quotations from Goethe, and found this line: "For a man remains of consequence not so far as he leaves something behind him but so far as he acts and enjoys, and rouses others to action and enjoyment."

Pepi Lederer was born Josephine Rose Lederer, on March 18, 1910, in Chicago. When she was a little girl, she was nicknamed Peppy because of her high spirits. In 1928, she changed the spelling to "Pepi" and made it her real name. At the time of her birth, her father, George Lederer, was producing popular musical comedies in Chicago. Her mother divorced him soon after Pepi was born. I remember her talking about her father only once, and that was in connection with the fact that he was Jewish, which she did not like. He died in 1938, in New York, at the age of seventy-seven. Her mother also died in 1938, in Beverly Hills, at the age of fifty-one. She was born Reine Douras, the eldest of four beautiful sisters, and was the first to use the name Davies in the theatre. She sang in vaudeville and musicals up to 1918, when her sister Marion began her association with Hearst and was able to support the three sisters and Pepi's brother, Charlie, in a big Beverly Hills house, on Lexington Road. Pepi saw her mother as seldom as possible. Only by accident did she feel compelled to speak to me about her. It was in January, 1930, when Pepi was living alone in a furnished apartment at 42 West Fifty-fourth Street, in a building owned by Mr. Hearst. One afternoon, I stopped in to see her and found her weeping, racked with guilt. Her mother had just left, she said, after storming uninvited into the apartment and making a terrible drunken scene. Pepi said that her mother had called Marion a scheming bitch for having robbed her of her children. She, Reine, was the first and the most beautiful of of the Davies sisters! And she, Reine, was going to make Marion pay and pay and pay till the day she died!

I was twenty-one and Pepi was seventeen when we first met, in 1928, on New Year's Day, at San Simeon. My husband, Eddie Sutherland, the film director, and I had been asked by Marion and Mr. Hearst to spend a week at "the ranch," as San Simeon was known, because cattle were still bred there and Mr. Hearst's mother's white frame house still stood on the grounds which covered thirty-two miles of seacoast. After three days, Eddie said to me, "I'll be damned if I'll be rousted out of the hay by a cowbell at eight o'clock every morning for breakfast, and have my liquor rationed as if I were some silly schoolboy. Besides, there's not even a golf course here. I'm going back to Hollywood tonight." Eddie was right to the extent that the ranch was a deadly-dull place for anyone who did not revel in opulence, who was not a member of Marion's stock company of guests, who was not mentally stimulated by visiting celebrities, and who wanted neither film advancement nor financial aid from Marion or Mr. Hearst. But Eddie had not, as I had, been initiated into Pepi's private world—a world of action utterly opposed to Marion's passive world, in which people literally sat and talked themselves to death. Pepi's world was a creation of her mind, needing no material setting; she carried it with her wherever she went. However, I felt that it was my duty as a wife to return to Hollywood with Eddie after he told Marion that urgent business recalled him to the Paramount studio. While he was asking her to arrange for a car to take us down to the train at San Luis Obispo, Pepi joined us and said to me, "Why do you have to go with Eddie? You have nothing to do in Hollywood." I stayed on for nearly three weeks.

To me, the most wondrously magnificent room in the castle was the great dining hall. I never entered it without a little shiver of delight. High above our heads, just beneath the ceiling, floated two rows of many-colored Sienese racing banners dating from the thirteenth century. In the huge Gothic fireplace between the two entrance doors, a black stone satyr grinned wickedly through the flames rising from logs propped against his chest. The refectory table seated forty. Marion and Mr. Hearst sat facing each other in the middle of the table, with their most important guests seated on either side. The morning after Eddie left, I was moved from a seat near Mr. Hearst to the seat next to Pepi at the bottom of the table, where she ruled. The other guests called us the Younger Degenerates. There were seven of us: Pepi; her brother Charlie; Sally O'Neil, the actress; Billy Haines, the actor; Lloyd Pantages, son of the theatre-owner; Chuck Crouch, a hanger-on; and me. Exactly ten minutes before dinner was announced, cocktails were served in the assembly hall. Anyone who dared to gulp down two in this time span was treated to an unforgettably frosty stare from Mr. Hearst, who did his best to curb Marion's drinking. However, at dinner we could drink all the champagne we pleased. Our waiter was a big, smiling cowboy kept in constant motion by Pepi with the order "Another bottle of champagne, my good man."

Because she was then the only fixed reality in an endless procession of celebrities at the ranch, Pepi could break any Hearst-Davies law and go unpunished. She never doubted that she would be found out. Guests, employees, servants—all were informers. But she had the knack of exposing people's vanities with a deftness that tickled everyone. The actress Claire Windsor's false bosom and the writer Madame Elinor Glyn's red wig would vanish from their bedrooms while they lay trustingly asleep. An "exclusive" item would appear in Louella Parsons' syndicated Hearst movie column which would later have to be retracted. Down the hill from the castle was an immense, clover-shaped marble swimming pool, spotted with statues and fountains. At noon one day, before Marion and Mr. Hearst were onstage, we were swimming in the pool when Pepi learned that a group of Hearst editors, solemnly outfitted in dark business suits, was sitting at the table, loaded with bottles of Scotch and gin, in the dining room of the Casa del Mar—the second-largest of three villas surrounding the castle. Pepi organized a chain dance. Ten beautiful girls in wet bathing suits danced round the editors' table, grabbed a bottle here and there, and exited, leaving one of the astonished men to inquire of a Hearst employee, Harry Crocker, "Does Mr. Hearst know these people are here?" The liquor controls imposed by Mr. Hearst were not easily circumvented. Marion's gin bottles (hidden in bathrooms) and the guests' whiskey bottles (hidden under mattresses) were often discovered and confiscated by snooping maids. Only Pepi had no liquor difficulties, because she had a private bootlegger. Joseph Willicombe, Mr. Hearst's executive secretary, had the keys to the wine vaults, and he could never resist Pepi's sparkling blue eyes and flashing smile. One night, while the proper guests were tucked away in the movie theatre in the castle, Pepi brought her "dainty group" together with three bottles of brandy in the living room of the Casa del Monte—the largest of the three villas. Rose Van Cleve, another of Marion's sisters, was there, too, curled up in the corner of a couch, sipping her drink and speaking to nobody, watching Pepi pounding out with her feet the beat of a Duke Ellington record playing on the phonograph. At midnight, Pepi, Lloyd, and I went to the kitchen in the castle to raid the ice-boxes. Quite unaccountably, Pepi flew into a rage and heaved great platters of cold cuts (prepared for lunch next day) all over the kitchen. The next time we tried a raid, we found the refrigerators padlocked.

On the last night of my stay at San Simeon, the Younger Degenerates produced their famous play *The Magoos*. The audience sat in the morning room, which faced the arched vestibule, which itself was separated from the dining hall by a wrought-iron gate. The gate was masked by green velvet draperies, which converted the vestibule into our stage. The play was a rustic piece written by Charlie Lederer. Chuck Crouch and Lloyd Pantages were Father and Mother Magoo. Charlie and Pepi Lederer were their innocent children. I was the bad girl, and Billy Haines was the bad man who came to rob them of their innocence. Sally O'Neil was the good fairy who flew in at the climax of the drama to save Pepi from Billy's lustful advances. The applause at the end of *The Magoos* was enthusiastic, chiefly because Pepi was a powerful, big girl and, in resisting Billy's advances, knocked him about with somewhat damaging results. Mr. Hearst suggested that Charlie rewrite the end of the play, flying Sally in to save Billy.

In February, Pepi asked me to spend a weekend at Marion's beach house, in Santa Monica, while Eddie and the director Wesley Ruggles were playing golf in Del Monte. That Saturday, I was kept late at the studio and did not arrive at the beach house till after dinner. As my car passed through the gateway, swung into the crescent drive, and stopped before the great double doors of the entrance hall, I had the eerie sensation of having at one moment left a palace shining with light and returned the next moment to find it so dark and still and lifeless that the shining palace seemed only a dream. There were no cars pulling out ahead of me or pulling up in the rear. There were no people talking and laughing as they entered the open doors to be greeted by Marion and Mr. Hearst standing just inside the hall. Before I could find a bell, a maid opened one of the double doors, took my dressing case, and told me that

Marion and Pepi were in the library. The crystal chandeliers in the long hall were not lighted. Entering the library, I saw, instead of the fairy princess, Marion sitting in a blue wrapper playing solitaire. Pepi, secure in her private world, was unchanged. The library was her favorite room in the beach house, because it contained a big Capehart record player, whose volume, when full up, compared favorably with that of a church pipe organ. She was playing the Paul Whiteman recording of "When Day Is Done" and wearing an intense ritual expression as she pounded out its beat. The maid brought me a tray of sandwiches, and I wondered whether, besides her and Marion and Pepi and me, and the night watchman passing through the dark hall with his flashlight, there was anyone in the house. Mr. Hearst was in New York on business.

When I finished a sandwich, we decided to play hearts, but the game was without interest, because none of us cared much for cards. After a while, Marion put down her hand and said to me, as if she were resuming an interrupted conversation, "One time when W.R. and I were going to New York, we got off the train in Chicago to get on the Twentieth Century Limited, and just then a train across the platform was also unloading and Mrs. Hearst got out of one of the cars. We all stared at each other for a second, and then W.R. went over to talk to her, leaving me standing there alone, and she gave me such a look of contempt—I could have killed her." Then Marion picked up her cards and went on with the game, while I tried to figure out why she, who knew me so casually, should tell me about this deeply wounding incident. Ten minutes later, she put down her cards again and asked me sharply, "Were you in *Louie the 14th* with Maybelle Swor?" I said "yes." She went on to ask me questions about Maybelle—whether, for instance, Mr. Hearst might be seeing her now in New York. I was very angry at finding myself placed in such an ugly position and would not answer. Through her personal spies, Marion knew far more about Mr. Hearst's affair with Maybelle than I did. Besides, for no apparent reason, since Maybelle was an unemployed chorus girl, her photograph appeared frequently in the Hearst newspapers; and she had once been painted by Henry Clive for the cover of Hearst's magazine the *American Weekly*. And it was certainly no secret that in New York she occupied a suite a few floors below the Hearst-Davies apartment at the top of his Warwick Hotel.

Marion's questions to me were based on Mr. Hearst's trip to New York in June, 1925, when Ziegfeld's *Louie the 14th* was playing at Hearst's Cosmopolitan Theatre. She took it for granted that I was one of the girls in that show who had been invited, along with Maybelle, to a party given on Mr. Hearst's yacht *Oneida*. I was too angry to tell Marion that I had left *Louie* in April, to begin rehearsals for the summer edition of the *Ziegfeld Follies*. To be a true Marionite, one had to hold the belief that Mr. Hearst had been to bed with no other woman since he met her. Obviously, I did not believe this, and she suspected me of having more than hearsay knowledge regarding the matter. After staring down at the table in a short reverie, she got up and said good night. Pepi and I watched her walk down the hall and up the Georgian staircase. It looked like a scene in the lobby of a deserted movie theatre. Watching her, too, were the almost life-size paintings following her along the wall of the hall and up the wall of the staircase—Marion in *When Knighthood Was in Flower*, in *Little Old New York*, in *Yolanda*, in *Janice Meredith*, in *Beverly of Graustark*, in *The Red Mill*, in *Quality Street*. . . .

Early in April, when Eddie was again away and Pepi asked me to spend another weekend at the beach house, it had returned to its dream state. On Saturday, there were twenty people to lunch; forty were added in the afternoon, to swim in the Venetian pool of white marble that separated the house from the ocean; and forty more were added for the buffet supper served on the porch overlooking the pool. It was understood that guests attending all-day parties should be gone by midnight. But it was much later when I asked Jack Pickford, Mary's brother, with whom I had been sitting in a porch swing, to take me to my room. Evidently, the night watchman had found it empty and locked it. Jack's car and chauffeur were waiting for him, so I went to his house to spend the night. Sunday afternoon, I returned home to learn from my sixteen-year-old brother, Theodore, who was visiting me from Wichita, Kansas, that Pepi had been playing Sherlock Holmes all day. At noon, she had knocked on my bedroom door at the beach house. When she got no answer and found it locked, she went outside and discovered a ladder, left by a workman, leaning against the roof of the porch. She climbed it and entered my room through a window. The bed had not been slept in. She telephoned Theodore to pick her up in his roadster, and, in search of me, he drove her to the homes of certain producers, stars, and directors selected from Marion's guest list. By Monday morning, everybody in Hollywood, including Eddie and Jack's girlfriend, Bebe Daniels, knew that I had spent the night with Jack Pickford.

This minor scandal had nothing to do with my filing suit for divorce from Eddie in May of 1928. I had married Eddie in July, 1926, because he was a charming man who had besieged me with the gold band. He belonged heart and soul to Hollywood; I was an alien there. He loved parties; I loved solitude. In October, 1927, I went to New York to visit Peggy Fears and her husband, A. C. Blumenthal. One night, Peggy, Blumie, Joe Schenck, and I went to Harry Richman's nightclub. Feeling bored, I excused myself to go to the ladies' room and went upstairs to the bar, where Helen Morgan was singing on top of her piano. George Marshall, the Washington businessman and owner of the Redskins—a man I had known for some years—was there and bought me a drink. It was the most fateful encounter of my life.

George Preston Marshall was born in 1896. When he was twenty-two, his father died, leaving him a small laundry in Washington, D.C., which, by the time he sold it in 1946, had been expanded into the Palace Laundry chain with fifty-seven branches. Running this dull business occupied very little of his time and a very small part of his brilliant mind. He was passionately fond of the theatre and films, and would have become an inspired producer if he had not found professional football a greater challenge. In 1932, he bought the Boston Braves football team and, with imaginative skill, turned that shabby team into the stunning Washington Redskins. I had first met George when I was eighteen and opened in *Louie the 14th* in Washington, in February, 1925. He was a tall, black-haired man of twenty-eight with a handsome face that was already marked by a subtle play of cruelty. After a party at the Shoreham Hotel, he took me, somewhat drunk, to my room at the Willard Hotel. We had been there only a few minutes when there was a knock at the door. George ran into the bathroom and hid behind the shower curtain, while I opened the door to the house detective. He went directly into the bathroom and came out with George. They chatted pleasantly, leaving the room together after the detective accepted a twenty-dollar bill from George. Half an hour later, when I was in bed, a woman employee came into the room and told me to get up, get dressed, and get out of the hotel. Since I was leaving Washington on the morning train for New York, I played dead till she grew tired of shaking me and went away.

When George and I met again, in 1927 I fell in love with his mind, which was panoramic. He concentrated absolutely on the business at hand, whether it was reading a comic strip or dipping into Le Sage's *The Devil on Two Sticks*. He understood my passion for books, which has made me perhaps the best-read idiot in the world. (Six years before he died, in 1969, he lost his mind after a stroke. I would not believe it. Every few months, I would call his secretary in

Washington, who would tell me again that George was "senile.") According to George, it was my truthfulness that made him fond of me, because truthfulness is a form of courage. And it was his obsession with his own cowardice that made him turn from art to rousting-about a team of brave men on the football field.

During that fragrant month of October, 1927, spent with George in New York, I was aware of a security I had never known before. From the outside, his life looked like a strenuously disordered striving among conflicting ambitions. It was in fact as perfectly ordered as a Carmelite nun's. I was determined, however, to forget him when I returned to Hollywood. It turned out that I could not, and we met as often as I was able to get away from the studio. Then, in April, 1928, as he was putting me on the train in Washington, he said, "Now, the first thing you must do, Scrubbie, when you get back to Hollywood is to start divorce proceedings against Eddie."

Eddie reacted to the news of my divorce proceedings with a series of scenes, ended by my removal to the Beverly Wilshire Hotel, two days after which Dr. Crispin telephoned me to say that Eddie's houseboy had found him in a stupor on the living-room floor. He had drunk a quart of whiskey and swallowed an assortment of pills. Although he had been very sick, he was recovering. A week later, I sent my maid back to the house to collect some forgotten knickknacks, and she returned to report that his friend Jimmie Cromwell was Eddie's houseguest. Aided by a flow of parties and pretty extra girls, Cromwell had brought about Eddie's full recovery.

Pepi's first reaction to my divorce proceedings was also not sanguine. Entrusting my fate to George Marshall she thought was madness. However, by the time the day of my divorce hearing arrived—June 19—she had become absorbed in her role as my witness. She had rehearsed several versions of Eddie's "mental cruelty," the ground upon which I was to receive my interlocutory decree. As we drove to court, my lawyer, Milton Cohen, selected her mildest version and begged her to subdue her performance and not to wink at the judge when she completed her testimony. She managed to restrain herself. Back in my suite at the Beverly Wilshire, after a shaker of Bacardi cocktails, she decided that Eddie, who was staying at the ranch, should be informed of the hearing. She sat down at the secretary and composed a telegram to him, ending with the line "You are now free to diddle with little or no compunction," and signed it with my name. Joe Willicombe received the telegram in his office at San Simeon. He gave it to Marion and Mr. Hearst, who passed it on to Eddie, who read it to everybody, who pronounced me a heartless adulteress who should be stoned.

That July, Pepi sailed for Europe with Marion and Mr. Hearst. In October, I sailed for Europe with George. He had telephoned me from Washington in September, the day before I was to sign for the fourth year of my Paramount contract, saying that the director Monta Bell had informed him that B. P. Schulberg would not give me the raise stipulated in my contract, and that therefore I was free to accept an offer I had received from the German director G. W. Pabst to make a picture called *Pandora's Box,* in Berlin. Neither of us had heard of Pabst before, or of the Frank Wedekind play *Pandora's Box,* on which the film was to be based. George's concern at the moment, though, was not my career but his need for a relaxing trip to Europe. When, some weeks later, George saw the first rushes of *Pandora's Box,* he said, "Scrubbie, you're great!" Aside from George and Pabst, nobody for the next twenty-five years seemed to hold this opinion.

After making *Pandora's Box* and another Pabst film, *Diary of a Lost Girl,* in Berlin, and Augusto Genina's *Prix de Beauté,* in Paris, I returned to New York in December, 1929, to find Pepi living not in a suite at the Warwick but at that hideous, red-wallpapered furnished apartment at 42 West Fifty-fourth Street. She explained that she was doing self-inflicted penance for having upset Marion and Mr. Hearst in Hollywood. It had all come about because of a most original weekend party she gave at the Beverly Hills house, on Lexington Road, when Charlie and Marion's sisters Rose and Ethel were conveniently absent. At the time, King Vidor was shooting *Hallelujah* with an all-Negro cast at M-G-M. On impulse, while visiting the set on the last day of production, she invited the vivacious little Nina May McKinney and some other members of the cast to the house on Lexington Road. After three days, a neighbor, shocked by the sight of black people running in and out of the mansion, telephoned Marion, who sent Ethel to end the party. At this point in the story, Pepi began to laugh, dropping any show of remorse. "And I shall never forget the expression on Ethel's face when she opened my door and saw me in bed with Nina May," Pepi said.

In January, 1930, Pepi gave me a more truthful explanation of why she had come to New York and was mortifying herself with red wallpaper. Secretly, she had yearned to be a movie actress, and when, in 1927, Sam Wood gave her a little comedy part in Marion's picture *The Fair Co-ed*, she was wild with delight. During filming, everyone said she was very good, but when the picture was released her part had been cut out, and Marion consoled her with the promise of a better part in her next picture. Six "next" pictures had been made since then, and now Pepi realized that no one had been really serious about her career—it was just a gag. While she was telling me this, we were packing her clothes in preparation for moving her back to the Warwick Hotel. Then the telephone rang. It was Marion calling from San Simeon. When Pepi hung up, she cried, "Quick, Watson, the needle!" and dashed off to the apartment of the actress Alma Rubens, in the same building.

Alma Rubens had starred in several pictures for Mr. Hearst, her last being *The Rejected Woman*, released through Metro-Goldwyn in 1924. Since then, her addiction to morphine had made work almost impossible, and Mr. Hearst, with Marion's approval, was supporting her. Pepi was much sobered when, after an hour, she returned from Alma's apartment. She had to wait till one of Marion's doctors came to give Alma an injection of morphine. Pepi had found her pacing up and down like a madwoman. All her money had gone to the drug-sellers; a mink coat that Marion had given her had gone to the pawn-broker; and her own doctor had refused to attend her further on credit. "She's nothing anymore," Pepi said. "Nothing but two big black terrified eyes." (Alma died a year later, on January 21, 1931.)

I had sublet an old-fashioned apartment, with three fireplaces and a fine library, on Park Avenue at Fifty-sixth Street. Occasionally, when George was in New York, he would spend a night there. My divorce had become final in June, 1929. After a financial settlement, George's wife was in the process of divorcing him. But he had given up all thoughts of marrying me after I had an affair with another man, in 1929. He had repossessed me for reasons of pride and jealousy, but now, viewed in a sensible light, I threatened to become an expensive burden. I had made two thousand dollars a week in Europe and returned to New York with three thousand dollars in the bank. I had infuriated him when I would not sign a contract with the newly organized RKO studio, because fifty percent of my value in his eyes lay in my being a movie star. Worst of all, he told me with careless truthfulness, the excitement of making love to a married woman was no longer present. (George married Corinne Griffith, the former movie star, in 1936. They separated in the forties, then divorced.)

George and I were having breakfast in my apartment one February morning when Pepi burst in, fired with a new project. A friend of the family, the newspaper publisher Ned McLean, had offered her his duck blind near Brooke, Virginia, as a retreat for a week where she could cut out liquor and could diet to the verge of anemia. This good thing she would do, she said, if I would go with her. "Absolutely not," I said. "If you think I'm going to have you on my hands alone for a week in the backwoods of Virginia, you're crazy." George thought otherwise. He was going to Palm Beach for a week and said he would feel better if I went someplace, too.

Pepi and I took the train to Washington, where we spent the night at Ned McLean's town house before being driven to his duck blind, about forty miles south, on the Potomac River. His town house was the notorious house on I Street where Edward Beale McLean, publisher of the Washington *Post*, had entertained Warren G. Harding, President of the United States from 1921 to 1923. It was a dark, secret house—a house of night, in which it was easy to imagine a bunch of men smoking cigars and drinking bourbon, sweating around the poker table, and entertaining the capital's most costly and discreet whores. Two big men in shirtsleeves let us into the house, and served our dinner in a comfortable fashion, giving us appraising looks and comparing impressions as they carried dishes in and out of the dining room. We might have heard what they said if there had not been, perched at opposite ends of the room, two white-crested cockatoos whose screams and squawks would have drowned out a brass band. After dinner, one of the men showed us upstairs to the master bedroom, where Pepi and I went to sleep in the most enormous bed we had ever seen.

Mr. Lee, Ned McLean's bachelor cousin from across the Potomac, in Virginia, welcomed us to the duck blind, which was an unpretentious brown wooden structure containing the usual living room, dining room, and kitchen downstairs. Upstairs, to Pepi's surprised delight, in the big bedroom over the living room, was the mate to the bed in the town house. Mr. Lee came over each morning to supervise the Negro servants and the stableboy. He was a man of about fifty, completely charming. We became friends at once, because he could smell the Kansas corn in my hair. But Pepi, that worldly imp, had never before met a Southern gentleman, and she didn't believe in him. She called him "Massa Lee" and talked to him with an outrageous Southern accent, to which he paid no mind. In fact, Pepi hated the country. Granted, the first two days of our visit were soured by her lack of liquor and rich food, but during the whole of our visit she never left the house. While Mr. Lee and I rode horseback, and boated on the Potomac, she rolled about the enormous bed or kept the Victrola in the living room at work on Bing Crosby's recording of "Mississippi Mud." On the day of our arrival, she had firmly ordered Mr. Lee to lock the liquor closet each night once he and I had drunk a Scotch-and-soda before he went home. When he had gone the second night, Pepi turned off the Victrola, went into the kitchen, where she ate some cold chicken and half an apple pie, and then went to the liquor closet.

"What do you know!" Pepi cried indignantly. "Massa Lee has locked the liquor closet!"

"You *told* him to lock it," I said.

"I'll fix that," she muttered, and she went again to the kitchen, returned with a hatchet, and, with three hefty chops, opened the door. For the rest of the week, she was happy, obliterating the countryside with Ned McLean's best rye whiskey, stuffing herself on delicious Southern cooking, and playing "Mississippi Mud."

When we returned to New York, she asked me to meet Ned McLean. He kept a suite at the Ritz, and one afternoon we went there for cocktails. He was extremely tall, with loping movements and a spoiled, boyish face. Pepi conducted the conversation, which brought him to life only when we discussed the difficulty of finding unregistered names for his racehorses.

Leaving the Ritz, on our way to a more enjoyable drink at the restaurant "21," Pepi said, "Ned wants me to ask whether you will go to Florida with him."

"Tell him, 'No, thank you,' " I said, and forgot him.

At "21," a beautiful boy came to our table, introduced himself, and sat down. He was Pare Lorentz, who was the film critic on the New York *Evening Journal*, a Hearst paper. Pepi was giving me a lesson to correct my "covered wagon" accent—seriously, but at the same time imitating one of her former English teachers. "No, no, Mary Louise, you 'rout' the enemy but you follow a 'route.' And it is 'Ballad of Reading Gaol' as in 'jail,' not 'gale.' " Then came the restoration of the final "t."

" 'Left,' 'kept,' 'slept,' " I pronounced correctly.

"Yes, but incorrectly arranged, Mary Louise. To be quite accurate, you should say 'slept,' 'kept,' 'left.' "

Pare thought Pepi was fascinating. When we rose to leave, he asked her for a date, and she became suddenly self-conscious and evasive.

Alone outside "21," I said to her, "Why in hell didn't you give Pare a date? He's a darling."

"He works for Mr. Hearst, doesn't he?" she said. "That's the only reason he wants a date with me."

At the end of March, I stopped by the Warwick to see Pepi and found her in bed, sick, feverish, and frightened. She had had an abortion and was hemorrhaging badly. This was the most astonishing piece of news since the Virgin Birth, because, as far as I knew, she had never gone to bed with any man. She explained that she had not menstruated for three months and finally, desperate for a reason, had told Marion about her condition on the telephone the day before yesterday. Marion told her to stop wasting time searching for a reason—to make an appointment to see an abortionist at once. He found that Pepi was pregnant, and aborted the fetus the next day.

"And you honestly don't know who the man was?" I asked, in consternation.

"No, I don't," she said violently. "And I don't want to know the name of a man who would rape a dead-drunk woman. It had to happen on New Year's Eve, when I got so drunk at a party given by Lawrence Tibbett that somebody had to take me home to the apartment on Fifty-fourth Street. But I don't remember who it was—and I don't want to remember who it was. And that's the end of it." (In 1935, after Pepi was dead, a mousy, deranged friend of hers told me with smiling satisfaction that it was he who had taken her home on that 1929 New Year's Eve and raped her. He added that whenever he had the opportunity he escorted his drunk women friends home and performed in the same manner.)

The first of June, 1930, brought Marion and Mr. Hearst to New York for three weeks of entertaining before they sailed for Europe. I was invited to a birthday party given for sister Rose at the Ritz. George Marshall was in town and took me to the party at ten o'clock. The maître d'hôtel was waiting for me at the entrance to the dining room. "I'm sorry, Miss Brooks, but the party has been postponed," he said. We could hear the music and see the people dancing in the Japanese Garden beyond the dining room. George laughed, I turned scarlet, and we went away. The next day, Pepi came to my apartment to confess that she had done me a frightful wrong. A year ago, she said, Rose had set herself up, in competition with Marion, as the mistress of her own wealthy, married, famous publisher, Ned McLean; and her musical-comedy portrayal of a fin-de-siècle courtesan had disgusted Pepi, who observed that whenever Ned was sober enough for action, he would strike out across country in an effort to get away from his paramour. He had been temporarily alone at the Ritz when he telephoned Pepi and asked her to introduce him to me. "So you see how things happen," she said. "I got in a fight with Rose night before last, and I couldn't resist telling her that Ned had asked you to go to Florida with him. She hit the ceiling, but I didn't know till this morning that she had barred you from the party. Marion and Mr. Hearst feel terrible about it, and they want me to bring you back to the Warwick for dinner."

Mr. Hearst was not the ogre depicted by Marion. He did not devour pretty girl guests; he loved them. At San Simeon, I had run away from him twice— once when he came upon me drying my hair by the pool, and once when he found me looking at a rare edition of Dickens in the library—because his marked attention would result in banishment by Marion from the ranch and from Louella Parsons' powerful movie column. Contrary to her reputation for being a gracious, generous friend, Marion was actively jealous of any pretty girl who caught Mr. Hearst's eye.

I was staying with Peggy and Blumie in Larchmont when Pepi telephoned to ask me to come to New York for the dinner at the Warwick, on the Friday preceding the midnight sailing of the *Olympic* on June 21. She was going to Europe with Hearst and Marion. Blumie sent Bert, his black chauffeur, and me to town in his silver Rolls-Royce town car. It was a dull dress-up, sit-down dinner. On my right was Albert Kobler, a small, elderly Hearst executive, who told me that he lived in a triplex apartment on Park Avenue—"with a Rembrandt in every corner." Like all sailing parties of the period, it was very drunken, and as I was about to get into Blumie's Rolls to be driven to the pier for final farewells on board the *Olympic,* I was stopped by another small, elderly man, who was drunk, and who demanded angrily, "What do you mean by trying to get into this car? I am Marion Davies' father! I am Judge Douras! And I know one of Marion's cars when I see it, and this is Marion's car." In the end, Bert persuaded the Judge to allow me to ride with him in "Marion's car" to the pier. On the promenade deck, I joined a crowd of spellbound passengers watching Marion and Dorothy Mackaill and Eileen Percy drunkenly dancing, with linked arms and high kicks, an old *Ziegfeld Follies* routine, which was brought to a finish by Marion's maid, who dragged her from the scene. I left the ship without attempting to find Pepi to say good-bye.

After our eleven o'clock show at the Capitol Theatre on Monday night,

April 15, 1935, my ballroom dance partner, Dario, and I found Pepi waiting backstage with Monica Morris and a huge basket of roses. She and Monica had arrived in New York that morning, and had come to invite us to supper at the Ritz Tower.

"Did you see the prologue?" I asked her.

"Part of it," she said indifferently, impatiently. "Now, please hurry and dress, because there are people waiting for us at the hotel." As I dressed, I said to myself, "Of course she's changed—it's been five years since I've seen her. She's grown up; she's twenty-five years old. But why should she rush to meet me with a basket of roses and then treat me with such irritability?" Waiting for us in the Ritz Tower were the comedienne Beatrice Lillie, the actor Roger Davis, and the beautiful Gloria Morgan Vanderbilt. I sat down with Gloria so that I could listen to her alluring soft Spanish lisp. (Her mother, Mrs. Harry Hays Morgan, was half Chilean, born in Santiago.) As sweetly as if she were reciting "The Owl and the Pussycat," she began telling me her story of how her ex-husband's sister, Mrs. Harry Payne Whitney, had obtained custody of both her daughter, little Gloria, and her five-million-dollar trust fund by charging big Gloria with an "ambiguous relationship" with Nada, Lady Milford Haven. While she talked, I watched Monica. She was small, dark, piquant, about thirty, her London accent pitched high as she exulted in her splendid situation and her approaching visit to "Mr. Hearst's castle at San Simeon." She was being briskly attentive to Bea Lillie, giving her a second Scotch-and-soda, after which, Bea rose from her chair to do a song-and-dance number with Roger and then sat down again for a prim, upright nap. Pepi was sitting with Dario, acting much more like her old self. He was a Hungarian immigrant, unaccustomed to the luxurious Hearst atmosphere, and Pepi was making him feel at home by listening sympathetically to the story of his life. When I joined them, he was telling her about his great success as a ballroom dancer. "When I finish Thursday at the Capitol, I am going to Louisville to dance for the week of the Kentucky Derby," he was saying.

Pepi looked at me through the long, straight fringe of her amber eyelashes. "Tell me, Miss Brooks, are you going to Kentucky to watch Dario dance?"

Back in New York, a couple of weeks later, while I was reading in bed at the Buckingham Hotel, Pepi telephoned asking whether she could come alone to see me at four o'clock. I said yes. At four I was gossiping on the telephone with Avis Golden, the daughter of the writer Rupert Hughes. With much laughter, I was telling her that last night had been a Mack Sennett comedy at the Ritz Tower, with Monica chasing me and Pepi chasing Monica from room to room. When I hung up, Pepi knocked at my door and came into the bedroom. She said that she had been standing in the hall for ten minutes listening to my conversation with Avis. "Everything you told Avis she will tell Marie Glendinning, who lives next door to her in Greenwich Village, and Marie will tell Marion," she said.

"And what," I asked, "have I told Avis that Marie and Marion do not already know?"

We were both furious, in quite different ways. Pepi was sitting on the side of my bed glaring at me with heavy menace, while I was pressed against my pillows glaring back with cold disdain. After a moment's deadlock, she got up and silently left the room. I later felt guilty about having made fun of her on the phone to Avis. I wanted to telephone her to say that I was sorry, but, in her drugged condition, she might become even more furious. So I packed my guilt with my dancing shoes and left that night for Kentucky, "to watch Dario dance."

Dario and I opened at the Persian Room of the Plaza on June 10, 1935. The next day, John McClain, a Hearst columnist and a close friend of mine, telephoned to say that he had just taken it off the wire service, that it would not be published, but that he felt he should tell me—Pepi had just killed herself by jumping out a window of the psychiatric section of the Good Samaritan Hospital in Los Angeles. Looking in the mirror as I checked my hair, makeup, and costume for the dinner show, I thought, her dreaded visit to Hollywood had lasted exactly six weeks.

Five days after Pepi's funeral Monica arrived in New York. She telephoned, asking me to meet her at Tallulah Bankhead's suite in the Gotham, so that she might tell me about Pepi's death. I found her alone, clad in black and suitably insulated with cocaine, prepared to make the most of the only part she would ever play in the world of celebrities. She had almost eliminated Pepi from the tragedy, and I heard nothing more than scattered comments on the circumstances of her death, which I pieced together with what John McClain had told me. When Pepi and Monica reached California, they had gone to the Beverly Hills house. Marion and Mr. Hearst were at San Simeon, but no summons came for Pepi and Monica to join them there. Weeks passed. There were no glittering parties at the Beverly Hills house, and Monica grew increasingly bored with family life among the Davies relatives. Then, without warning, Marion and Mr. Hearst decided to have Pepi committed to the hospital for a drug cure. She had time only to slip her diamond ring from her finger to give to Monica before she was taken away. In the hospital, she was left alone by the nurse for a moment in a room with steel-mesh screening over the window. In an agony of desolation, this powerful one-hundred-eighty-pound woman must have taken a running dive at the window in order to tear through the screen, and she hit the ground with force enough (according to the autopsy) to fracture her spine and almost every other bone in her body.

"About the diamond ring, Monica?" I asked. "Didn't you know that it was Pepi's *one* precious possession—that it had never been off her finger since Marion gave it to her, on her eighteenth birthday? Weren't you suspicious when she gave it to you just before she was taken off alone to the psychiatric ward?"

"No—but it doesn't matter. They took it back from me. As soon as Marion and Mr. Hearst got word of Pepi's suicide, they had my trunk searched. A bundle of Pepi's letters to me was taken from it—fear of blackmail, no doubt. Then the diamond ring was snatched from my finger, and I was told that I was being deported immediately after the funeral." Monica laughed and gave a comforting pat to her handbag, which contained a Hearst-Davies steamship ticket to Southampton and a thousand dollars in cash. "But, do you know, you people in Hollywood are very comical—especially when you're pretending to be serious," she said. "Pepi's funeral service, in Mr. Hearst's private chapel, had begun when that tall, blond actress friend of Marion's, the one who gets up and makes funny speeches during dinner at the ranch—what's her name?"

"Katherine Menjou," I said.

"Yes," Monica said, laughing again. "This Katherine Menjou came down the chapel aisle wearing a white picture hat and a bouffant white dress covered with big black polka dots, smiling and waving to everyone as if she were greeting friends at a garden party. She quite stole the scene from poor old Pepi, lying there in her bronze casket."

FOUR | *Humphrey and Bogey*

Humphrey Bogart spent the last twenty-one years of his life laboriously converting the established character of a middle-aged man from that of a conventional, well-bred theatre actor named Humphrey to one that complemented his film roles—a rebellious tough known as Bogey. In the years since his death, in 1957, biographers catering to the Bogey Cult have transformed him into a cinematic saint—St. Bogart—in whom I can find scarcely a trace of the Humphrey I first knew in 1924 or the Bogey I last saw in 1943. The earliest strokes in the biographers' portraits are those that paint him as a "loner," a man of "self-determination," who makes "all his own decisions," with regard for nothing beyond immediate satisfaction. Such a description will not do for a twentieth-century film star in Hollywood. Being myself a born loner, who was temporarily deflected from the hermit's path by a career in the theatre and films, I can state categorically that in Bogart's time there was no other occupation in the world that so closely resembled enslavement as the career of a film star. He had self-determination only in this: he might or he might not sign a film contract. If he signed the contract, he became subject to those who paid his salary and released his films. If he did not sign the contract, he was no film star. I, for example, when I was under contract to Paramount in 1928, complained about being forced to hang around Hollywood waiting to make some film. "That's what we are paying you for—your time" was the harsh comment of the front office. "You mean my life," I said to myself. When the coming of talkies made the cutting of actors' salaries practicable and I was the only one on the Paramount lot who refused to take a cut, thereby losing my contract, I doubted whether such "independent" decisions would lengthen my career. When I was the only one of the cast who refused to return to make the talkie version of *The Canary Murder Case*, my last silent film there, the studio doused me with ugly publicity and made my doubts a certainty. I was blacklisted. No major studio would hire me to make a film. In later years, whenever Bogart, at Warner Brothers, followed the lead of James Cagney and Errol Flynn by going on strike and demanding better films and more money, the studio would make a pleasant game of it. The actors were allowed a triumphant interval in which to feel like lords of the lot; the publicity stirred up by these mock battles was free and beneficial; and a great deal of money was saved while the actors' salaries were suspended. Studio contracts were always a joke, as far as actors were concerned. Studios could break them at will; the actors were bound by their fear of impoverishing lawsuits and permanent unemployment.

As a loner, I count as my two most precious rights those that allow me to choose the periods of my aloneness and allow me to choose the people with whom I will spend the periods of my not-aloneness. To a film star, on the other hand, to be let alone for an instant is terrifying. It is the first signpost on the road to oblivion. Obviously, an actor cannot choose the people with whom he will work, or when or how he will work with them. He goes to work at a time specified by the studio. He spends his working day under the control not only of his director but also of the scriptwriter, the cameraman, the wardrobe department, and the publicity office. Since publicity is the lifeblood of stardom, without which a star will die, it is equally obvious that he must keep it flowing through his private life, which feeds the envy and curiosity that bring many people into theatres. Bogart, having rightly ascribed much of his previous failure in the theatre and films to a lack of publicity value, determined that from the moment he settled at Warner Brothers, in 1936, all his time not spent before the camera would be spent with journalists and columnists, who would invent for him the private character of Bogey. They carved him into the desired peg upon which they could hang their favorite ancient gags and barroom fables. A small part of Bogey's character was founded on his film roles; the greater part was founded on the pranks of those gangsters idolized by the film producer Mark Hellinger, who was an ex-columnist. During the last ten years of his life, Bogart allowed himself to be presented to the world by journalists as a coarse and drunken bully, and as a puppet Iago who fomented evil without a motive. He was neither.

In 1924, my first impression of Humphrey Bogart was of a slim boy with charming manners, who was unusually quiet for an actor. His handsome face was made extraordinary by a most beautiful mouth. It was very full, rosy, and perfectly modeled—perfectly, that is, except that, to make it completely fascinating, at one corner of his upper lip a scarred, quilted piece hung down in a tiny scallop. When Humphrey went into films, a surgeon sewed up the scallop, and only a small scar remained. Photographically, it was an improvement, but I missed this endearing disfigurement. The scar on his lip has since become a symbol of his heroism. In those early years, it was taken for granted that he got punched in the mouth at some speakeasy. When Humphrey drank, he became exhausted and occasionally fell asleep (as in *Casablanca*) with his head in his arms on the table. If he was abruptly shaken awake, he would say something rude and sometimes get socked for it. On one occasion, he purposely did not get his split lip sewed up, because he both loved and hated his beautiful mouth. America in the twenties was exclusively Anglo-Saxon in its ideas of beauty, and vulgar people made fun of Humphrey's "nigger lips." The lip wound gave him no speech impediment, either before or after it was mended. But when he at last made a hit in films, observing how much an unusual feature, such as Clark Gable's prominent ears, added to the publicity value of a star, he decided to exploit his mouth. Over the years, Bogey practiced all kinds of lip gymnastics, accompanied by nasal tones, snarls, lisps, and slurs. His painful wince, his leer, his fiendish grin were the most accomplished ever seen on film. Only Erich von Stroheim was his superior in lip-twitching. But in 1924 Humphrey, in New York, was speaking his lines with a well-projected baritone and good diction in a small part in a play called *Nerves*. Mary Philips also had a small part in *Nerves*. Kenneth MacKenna played a leading role. The play's nerves would have been a good deal shakier if the cast had known that after Humphrey married and was divorced by Helen Menken he would marry Mary Philips, and that after Kenneth married and was divorced by Kay Francis he would marry Mary Philips, who by then had divorced Humphrey.

In respect to future entanglements, the Broadway theatrical season of 1925–26 was even more arresting. James Cagney, who was to become Humphrey's redheaded bête noire at Warner Brothers, was playing in *Outside Looking In;* Leslie Howard, who was to put Humphrey in a position to rival Cagney, was playing in *The Green Hat;* Helen Menken was in *Makropoulos Secret;* Mary Philips was in *The Wisdom Tooth;* and Bogart's Wife Number 3, Mayo Methot, was in *Alias the Deacon.* In *The Cradle Snatchers*, Humphrey was playing a college boy being snatched by middle-aged Mary Boland, while offstage in the Bronx the year-old Lauren Bacall lay in her cradle waiting for Bogey to snatch her twenty years later as Wife Number 4.

From the 1921–22 season, when Humphrey first appeared on Broadway—with Alice Brady, in *Drifting*—through the 1929–30 season, when he got his first Hollywood contract, 2,044 plays were produced in New York. Out of perhaps two thousand young American dramatic actors working in those plays, only four besides Bogart became major film stars—Cagney, Spencer Tracy, Fredric March, and Clark Gable. Moreover, whether or not it is generally admitted as frankly as it once was by Barbra Streisand—she said, "To me being really famous is being a movie star"—that is the goal of all actors in the theatre.

In 1930, Humphrey's failure in Hollywood was as predictable as Cagney's success. Cagney's character was already a gaudy perfection in the theatre. In *Penny Arcade*, the play that won him his film contract with Warner Brothers, Cagney appeared as the same little hoodlum killer that made him famous in films. Bogart was selected out of *It's a Wise Child*, in which he played a gentlemanly young cad, and so had only his good looks to recommend him to Hollywood producers, who didn't know how to transform him into Bogey. Bogart used to refer to a review by Alexander Woollcott as his favorite among the reviews he had received while on the stage: it described his performance in *Swifty* as "inadequate." To be mentioned at all in any review amounted to praise for Bogart. On the stage, he was as formless as an impression lost through lack of meditation, as blurred as a name inked on blotting paper.

In the twenties, under the supervision of old producers like David Belasco, stage direction dated back to the feverish technique of the English theatre before the plays of Ibsen, Chekhov, and Bernard Shaw revolutionized it, introducing what Lytton Strachey called "a new quiet and subtle style of acting—a prose style." In New York, we began to realize how bad our directors and actors were when the new young English stars began to appear on Broadway. There was Lynn Fontanne in *Pygmalion*, Roland Young in *The Last of Mrs. Cheyney*, Leslie Howard in *Berkeley Square*, and Gertrude Lawrence and Noel Coward in *Private Lives*. These marvelous actors of realism spoke their lines as if they had just thought of them. They moved about the stage with ease. And they actually paid attention to—they actually *heard*—what other actors were saying. The conventional Broadway technique of that period exposed more showing off than acting, more of a fight than a play. Every actor's aim was to kill the other actors' lines—especially if the lines provoked laughter. Ina Claire was celebrated for waving a large chiffon handkerchief on other actors' lines and forcing them to work with their backs to the audience. Far from being criticized, she was envied for such tricks.

After thirteen years of conditioning by this kind of "stage" acting, when Bogart got a job in Robert Sherwood's *The Petrified Forest*—starring Leslie Howard and directed by Arthur Hopkins—which opened in January, 1935, nothing but searching ambition could have enabled him to see in Leslie Howard's quiet, natural acting technique a style he could adapt to his own personality, a style that would prepare him for *The African Queen*. In that film he developed his character with his voice alone. Nothing but inflexible willpower could have enabled him to tear down his ingrained acting habits in order to submit all over again to the self-conscious agony of learning to act. Working with Leslie gave him command of the Duke Mantee part in the play and, later, in the film; but the films of the following five years reveal the terrible struggle for supremacy between the new Bogey technique and the old theatrical habits of Humphrey. With a poor director, Frank McDonald, in *Isle of Fury*, he was Humphrey again, reciting his memorized lines, striking attitudes while he waited for the other actors to get done with theirs. In *Dark Victory*, working with a great director, Edmund Goulding, who was also a great clown, and acting with the emotional Bette Davis, who could fire up on the word "camera," he was stricken with grotesque, amateur embarrassment. Unlike most technical actors, Humphrey was extremely sensitive to his director. But, like most actors from the theatre, he was slow in building a mood and grimly serious about maintaining it. Cagney, in *The Roaring Twenties*, threw him into confusion, splitting him between Bogey and Humphrey. Cagney's swift dialogue and his swift movements, which had the glitter and precision of a meat slicer, were impossible to anticipate or counterattack. Humphrey was at his best working with less inspired and more technical actors, such as Walter Huston. He was also at his best playing an inarticulate, uncomplicated character, like the punk in *San Quentin*. His senseless pursuit of death became pathetic, even noble, because it came out of his own indomitable perseverance in pursuing stardom. In *The Maltese Falcon* his part was uncomplicated, but too much dialogue betrayed the fact that his miserable theatrical training had left him permanently afraid of words. In short speeches, he cleverly masked his fear with his tricks of mouth and voice, but when, in this film, he was allotted part of the burden of exposition, his eyes glazed and invisible comic-strip balloons circled his dialogue. Even more unfortunate were his efforts at repartee with Mary Astor in *Across the Pacific*. In his last films, it was not the theatre Humphrey who overcame Bogey —it was the real man, Humphrey Bogart, whose fundamental inertia had always menaced his career. As a dead soul waiting for release in death in *The Desperate Hours*, he was incomparable until, unaccountably, a sentimental heart began to beat, and he handed over the film to Fredric March. However, before inertia set in, he played one fascinatingly complex character, craftily directed by Nicholas Ray, in a film whose title perfectly defined Bogart's own isolation among people. That film was *In a Lonely Place*. It gave him a role that he could play with complexity, because the film character's pride in his art, his selfishness, his drunkenness, his lack of energy stabbed with lightning strokes of violence were shared by the real Bogart. In his preface to *The Doctor's Dilemma*, Shaw wrote,

> No man who is occupied in doing a very difficult thing, and doing it very
> well, ever loses his self-respect. . . . The common man may have to found
> his self-respect on sobriety, honesty, and industry; but . . . an artist needs
> no such props for his sense of dignity. . . . The truth is, hardly any of us
> have ethical energy enough for more than one really inflexible point of
> honor. . . . An actor, a painter, a composer, an author, may be as selfish
> as he likes without reproach from the public if only his art is superb; and
> he cannot fulfil this condition without sufficient effort and sacrifice to make
> him feel noble and martyred in spite of his selfishness.

Superficially, Humphrey's character and way of life so little resembled those of the secure and temperate Leslie Howard that what induced Leslie to become his guide and champion is not immediately apparent, but Leslie did become both. I would never have known the reason for his sympathetic attitude toward Humphrey if I had not met Leslie in New York in November, 1931, when he was rehearsing his new play, *The Animal Kingdom.*

On the afternoon of my twenty-fifth birthday, my friend George Marshall announced that he was going to celebrate the event by taking me to dinner at the Casino in the Park with Leslie Howard and his wife. I was surprised and pleased, not only because George had been mad at me for turning down an offer to work for RKO in Hollywood but also because he so little liked spending unnecessary money on me. (The last time I spoke to him on the phone, in 1960, he was still wondering why he had given me a mink coat in 1928.)

Conversationally, the dinner party was not well balanced. When I was with George, I said little, fearing that I might give him material for an inquiry into how I spent my time when he was away in Washington. Leslie, who had evidently accepted the invitation because he enjoyed George's social performances, said nothing. Mrs. Howard, a large Englishwoman who looked more like Leslie's mother than his wife, tried to inject gracious remarks here and there into the stream of George's witty stories, but his loud voice was as hard on them as it was on Eddie Duchin's orchestra, playing in the background. George was a tall, physical man of thirty-five. At the end of each story, he would let out a self-appreciative haw-haw-haw and then clap Leslie on the back with such enthusiasm that Leslie crumpled over the table like a paper angel.

Dinner ended, George asked Mrs. Howard to dance, and Leslie and I were left alone at the table, regarding each other.

I opened the conversation: "I hate my dress. Bernard Newman at Bergdorf Goodman talked me into buying it, but it's much too young for me."

Leslie studied the dress—a lettuce-green organza evening gown, with a full skirt, short sleeves, and baby collar. I turned in my chair to show him a bow in back. "What do you usually wear?" he asked.

"Oh, something white and glittery, with no back and cut down to here in front."

He thought about this for a moment, and then we both laughed and had another glass of champagne. He had become suddenly, brilliantly alive. His famous watchful eyes began to sparkle mischievously as we compared our impressions of Hollywood. As much as I, he detested having to sit most of the day in the studio waiting for sets and lights to be changed. After that, he talked about the theatre—how he dreaded having to study a new part, how slow he was at learning his lines.

I laughed in disbelief. "You're kidding me!"

"No, it's perfectly true," he said. "I wasn't cut out to be an actor. I haven't the energy for acting—it's too exhausting."

When Mrs. Howard and George returned from their dance and observed our happy intimacy, they decided to take us home. In the cab, Mrs. Howard and I sat on the back seat, facing George and Leslie, on the jumpseats. My knees touched Leslie's, and we smiled at each other. But I knew when we said good night that I would not see him again. It would be too exhausting.

It was the recognition of this same threatening exhaustion in Humphrey, I think, that touched Leslie's heart, leading him to force Jack Warner to give Humphrey the Duke Mantee part when *The Petrified Forest* was filmed. Furthermore, whereas from the beginning of his career Leslie had confessed his lack of energy and let it work for him in the creation of the quiet, natural actor, he saw that Humphrey fought his weakness, trying ineffectually to emulate the dynamic style of most successful actors. The futility of this he conveyed to Humphrey in the direction of the play. And once Humphrey grasped the idea that he, too, might achieve success with some version of natural acting, he went about contriving it with the cunning of a lover. For all actors know that truly natural acting is rejected by the audience. Although people are better equipped to judge acting than any other art, the hypocrisy of "sincerity" prevents them from admitting that they, too, are always acting some role of their own invention. To be a successful actor, then, it is necessary to add eccentricities and mystery to naturalness, so that the audience can admire and puzzle over something different from itself. Leslie's eccentricities were his fondness for his pipe and for English tweed. Bogart's eccentricities were the use of his mouth and speech. As for mystery, Leslie would have become less if he had revealed himself; Bogart did reveal himself and became more.

Humphrey, according to his biographers, had an amazing number of "recreations." He played golf, tennis, bridge, chess. He sailed. He read *books!* Except on one occasion, the only thing I ever saw him do was sit drinking and talking with people. That one occasion was an evening in New York when he and I, Blyth Daly, and the actress Alice Brady played what Alice innocently called bridge, in her apartment on East Fifty-seventh Street. For one thing, Alice never stopped talking. Then, as soon as the cards were dealt, she would get up to mix drinks. After the bidding, she would get up to empty ashtrays. When she was dummy, she would go to the piano to play and sing in French—her mother's tongue. At any time at all, she would jump up, with all her bracelets jingling, to fly at one of her four yapping wire-haired fox terriers. We were relieved when her doorbell rang and Elsie Ferguson, with her handsome actor husband, came in for a nightcap after the theatre. The bridge game was over. Sipping a brandy across the room from me, Elsie was as beautiful in 1930 as she had been in films in 1918. And it was with the old film charm that she said good night a few minutes later, leaving Alice sitting on her husband's lap.

"How long have Alice and Elsie's husband known each other?" I asked Humphrey as we left the apartment building.

He looked at me blankly.

It was Blyth who answered, "You idiot, they just met!"

That blank look of Humphrey's was the key to his attitude toward sex. He was so contemptuous of other men's needs to publicize their amorous triumphs that he refused to notice them. Being supremely confident of his own attractiveness to women, he scorned every form of demonstrativeness. When a woman appealed to him, he waited for her the way the flame waits for the moth. "Man survives earthquakes, epidemics, the horrors of war, and all the agonies of the soul," wrote Tolstoy, "but the tragedy that has always tormented him, and always will, is the tragedy of the bedroom." It was security in sex that preserved Humphrey's ego until his eventual success after he had endured the bitterest humiliation, ridicule, and failure. Certainly no other actor could have read those two speeches in *Across the Pacific* with his peculiar emphasis. When Sidney Greenstreet showed him his gun, Bogey produced his and said, "My gun is bigger than your gun." And again, later, when he pulled his gun on Greenstreet, he said, "I told you—mine is bigger than yours."

Each of Humphrey's wives was fittingly chosen to accord with the progress of his career. When he began to act and had so much to learn about the theatre, he married Helen Menken, the star of *Seventh Heaven*. Helen's white, thin face was always ecstatically lifted up to her vision of the Drama. I never heard her talk about anything except the art of the theatre. They were divorced in 1927, after Helen had become a sensation in *The Captive*, which was closed by the District Attorney on its one hundred sixtieth performance because of its lesbian theme. Humphrey worked that year in the twelve pitiful performances of a comedy called *Baby Mine*, in which Roscoe "Fatty" Arbuckle tried to erase the scandal that had driven him from Hollywood. Except for a two-week revival of Maxwell Anderson's *Saturday's Children*, in 1928, Humphrey did not work again on Broadway until 1929, when, with his new wife, Mary Philips, he appeared in *Skyrocket*, which closed after eleven performances. "The art of the theatre" having become a sore subject, Mary was exactly right for him during that time, when he required comfort more than inspiration.

Except for Leslie Howard, no one contributed so much to Humphrey's success as his third wife, Mayo Methot. He found her at a time of lethargy and loneliness, when he might have gone on playing secondary gangster parts at Warner Brothers for a year and then been out. But he met Mayo and she set fire to him. Those passions—envy, hatred, and violence, which were essential to the Bogey character, which had been simmering beneath his failure for so many years—she brought to a boil, blowing the lid off all his inhibitions forever. Part of her mission was accomplished under my direct observation.

In October, 1935, I left my ballroom dance act with Dario Borzani at the Persian Room in New York to make a test for the Republic Studio in Hollywood for a film called *Dancing Feet*. On the day after the test was completed and seen, the studio gave the part I had tested for to a girl who couldn't dance. Having little money and no more faith in myself, I stayed on in Hollywood for lack of a better plan. I was living at the Ronda Apartments. One day, I strolled down the street to Robert Benchley's cottage at the Garden of Allah, and there was Humphrey sitting on the floor, leaning against a sofa, with a glass of

Scotch-and-soda in his hand. He had little to say about his part in *The Petrified Forest*, which was in production at Warner Brothers. Two unsuccessful experiences in Hollywood did not allow him to feel optimistic. Not feeling optimistic, either, was a boy from the M-G-M Studio who had been sent to pick up a script that Benchley had not yet begun to write, for one of his comedy short subjects. The boy watched Bob prepare for the typewriter with a glass of straight Scotch. It was almost impossible for anyone working on a Benchley film to stay sober, because he demanded that they keep pace with his drinking. The following evening, I received a phone call from the theatrical agent Mary Huntoon, who was an old friend of mine and a niece of Dwight Deere Wiman, the producer of *The Little Shows*, with songs by Rodgers and Hart. She said that Humphrey and she were having a drink at her house (she had just become his agent), and that Humphrey would like me to join them. Coming from anyone else, the invitation would have meant that two bored people wanted company. Coming from Humphrey, it was nothing less than a declaration of love. Full of curiosity, I hastened to the scene. It was not a happy one. Humphrey was so intuitive about women that, after a glowing welcome, he retreated slowly into gloom and silence and Scotch, leaving the conversation to Mary and me. Riding home in the cab, I thought about how different Humphrey and I were. He could love only a woman he had known a long time or—what amounted to the same thing—one who was flung at him in the intimacy of a play or film. To me, love was an adventure into the unknown.

By the time I next saw Humphrey, *The Petrified Forest* had been released and he had made a solid hit in it. It was early in 1936, at the Beverly Hills home of Eric Hatch, who had written the film *My Man Godfrey*. When I went into the dining room, Eric and his wife, Mischa Auer and his wife, and Humphrey were sitting at the table. Mrs. Hatch got up to pour me a cup of coffee. As I drank it, I watched Humphrey, whom I had never seen in such an emotional state. Everyone else was watching him, too. Then the doorbell rang, and, as if on cue, we all got up and went downstairs into the vaulted living room to meet Mayo Methot, who was entering from the hall, clad in a sheath of peacock-blue silk. That night, instead of having our usual talk and laughter, we became an audience galvanized by a scene of the most passionate love played out between Mayo and Humphrey without so much as a touch of hands. Drinks were mixed and seats were taken as Mayo moved restlessly to the phonograph and put on an old Argentine tango, "Adios Muchachos." She got up and danced with Mischa. The dance began as a burlesque, with him throwing her about and glaring lustfully into her eyes. Gradually, however, her exquisitely persuasive body began to rule his movements, and they danced in the falling arcs, the slow recoveries, and the voluptuous pauses of the true tango. The spell was broken by a maid, who announced that Mayo's husband had telephoned to say he was on his way to the house. Humphrey sprang from the sofa to whisk her away. But wait! She had taken off her slippers to dance, and now one of them could not be found. Everyone searched for it except me, and that must have aroused Humphrey's suspicions, because quite suddenly he lunged at me with the most hideous face, rasping, "God damn you, Louise, tell us where you hid Mayo's slipper!" I was too stunned by this strange and violent Humphrey to speak. Fortunately, at this moment Mischa stretched up to an oak beam, which no one else was tall enough to reach, and brought down the slipper. The lovers fled through the back door as the front doorbell rang.

It was in December of 1943, in New York, that I saw Humphrey for the last time. I was dining at the "21" Club with screenwriter Townsend Martin. Between the dinner and the supper hour, when the bar was empty, Mayo and Humphrey came in and stood briefly at our table to say hello and tell us that they were on their way to Africa to entertain the troops. I was shocked to see how dreadfully Humphrey's face had aged. The effects of the war he had waged against his inertia—work and whiskey without sleep and food—were visible at last. Mayo looked as though she had just got out of bed with her clothes on. Her suit was rumpled, her hair not combed, her face not made up. They sat at a table in a far corner of the room as if they wanted to be alone, yet they neither spoke nor looked at each other till their drinks were brought to the table. Then Mayo turned to speak fiercely to Humphrey, as if she were continuing some argument that could never be resolved. Slumped against the banquette, unmoved, he stared at his hand slowly turning his glass round and round on the table. It was plain that the team of "The Battling Bogarts" was soon to break up. He was Bogey now, his character firmly set, capable of battling alone. With the release of *Casablanca*, Humphrey Bogart had become big business. It was time for Lauren Bacall to make her entrance—she who was also to become his perfect screen partner, as seductive as Eve, as cool as the serpent.

My most vivid remembrance of the real Humphrey Bogart is of a night in New York at Tony's bar on Fifty-second Street. I went in at about one o'clock in the morning and sat at a table near Humphrey, who was sitting in a booth with the actor Thomas Mitchell. It was a few weeks before the

Broadway version of *The Petrified Forest* would close, in June, 1935. Humphrey had nothing to look forward to except summer stock in Skowhegan, Maine. Presently, Mitchell paid his bill and went out, leaving Humphrey alone, drinking steadily, with weary determination. His head drooped lower and lower. When I left, he had fallen into his exhausted sleep, with his head sunk in his arms on the table. "Poor Humphrey," I said to Tony. "He's finally licked."

My most vivid remembrance of the screen Humphrey Bogart is of a scene in John Huston's *The Treasure of the Sierra Madre*. He lies in the dirt, about to drag himself to the waterhole. He has endured everything to get his gold—and now must he give it up? Wide open, the tragic eyes are raised to heaven in a terrible, beseeching look. In the agony of that beautiful face I see the face of my St. Bogart.

Almost as cautiously as he won success in the theatre and films during the twenties, W. C. Fields won the hearts of American schoolboys during the sixties. A curious idol. For he had become their beloved not so much because they appreciated his comic art—based on the years of work he spent practicing juggling and perfecting his timing, which is almost the whole of comedy—as because they imagined him to be a character like Quilp in Dickens' *The Old Curiosity Shop*. Quilp fell on the floor and rolled with laughter when he forced Sampson Brass to drink boiling rum and water. Fields was supposed to have pleasured himself by spiking Baby Leroy's milk with a possibly lethal dose of gin. It is the word "work" that makes the schoolboys' love affair with Fields suspect. "Work" was not a word in their vocabulary, and Fields was perhaps the only comedian known to them who revealed, through his stately procedures, the passionate amount of work he put into his performance.

In the sixties, many schoolboys wrote to me and came to see me. Most of them knew only my name and had never seen any of my films. They approached me with wildly uninformed flattery, after which, presuming me to be a forlorn old actress full of gratitude, they expected me to fill their arms with my most precious still pictures and sit three hours at the typewriter composing material that they could muck about, sign with their names, and present to the teachers of their film classes. Where Fields was concerned, it did not take me long to learn that these boys had seen few of his films, for in discussing any one of them they had great difficulty remembering its title or whether they had seen the whole of it or an excerpted reel or two. The Fields they idolized was the man they read about and superimposed on the Fields they saw (or didn't see) on the screen.

In 1778, Samuel Johnson wrote, "Pointed axioms and acute replies fly loose about the world, and are assigned successively to those whom it may be the fashion to celebrate." In 1922, when I first arrived in New York, I heard all sorts of gags, jokes, and anecdotes, and over the past twenty years of reading I have been brought to a condition of nausea as I have found them "assigned successively" to various film celebrities. There are two categories of celebrities —fitted with appropriate anecdotes—that writers and readers appear to dote on with foolish, untiring enthusiasm. They are the tramp-type woman star delineated by her outrageous conduct and the drunken actor whose cruel antics are considered hilarious. In the first category is the star who, in the favorite anecdote, goes into a smart restaurant clad only in a mink coat and a pair of slippers. Beneath the coat she is naked! The question is, how is it known —her nakedness? Does she take the coat off? In that case, the management would swiftly bundle her into a waiting cab, and every newspaper across the country would carry the story. Journalists refer to the mink-coat anecdote as a "possible" item. It *could* happen. It probably has happened, but not to a star with the eyes of the press upon her. No documentation ever confirms this anecdote, which is usually assigned to some such star as Jean Harlow. Thomas Gray said, "Men will believe anything at all provided they are under no obligation to believe it." In the second category—the drunken actor, to whom are attached anecdotes out of the myths surrounding Irish wakes—writers have contrived an item so nearly impossible that no devoted reader about films doubts it for an instant. This *funny* story tells about a bunch of drunks who steal the body of an actor friend from his casket in a funeral home and set it up in a chair in another friend's house, during his absence. Surprise! I have consulted funeral directors and the police about this repulsive prank, and find that breaking into a funeral home would immediately arouse the forces of the law and get the pranksters clapped into jail. It is not necessary to add that such a frolic with the body of W. C. Fields would attract the notice of the press.

Where two or three are gathered together in his name, they do not waste time discussing W. C. Fields' films; they get right down to their "favorite stories" about "the little guy who looked life in the eye and told it where to go." With more than fifty years separating them from the Fields of the theatre and his unseen early films, his admirers must rely on the word of journalists like Roger Doughty, who has written, "Fields' characterization of a seedy, irascible, sharp-tongued drunk with a bulbous nose and an ice-cold heart made him a headliner in the *Ziegfeld Follies, George White's Scandals*, Earl Carroll's *Vanities* and such films as *Never Give a Sucker an Even Break* and *If I Had a Million.* . . . In later years he jousted with Charlie McCarthy on Edgar Bergen's radio show." The actual facts of Fields' character development are these: In 1923–24, he appeared on Broadway in the musical comedy *Poppy*. He played a small-time bungling cheat, an affectionate father with no trace of drunkenness. William LeBaron saw *Poppy*, and in 1925, after he had become head of production at Paramount's Long Island studio, he gave Fields a contract. *If I Had a Million* was released in 1932. Fields worked on Edgar Bergen's radio show in 1937 and 1938. *Never Give a Sucker an Even Break* was released in 1941. Another writer, Jim Harmon, quotes Bergen as saying,

"Fields would be drinking in the morning, drinking at noon, drinking in the afternoon. But he *never* acted as if he were drunk." On his own, Harmon goes on to call Fields "a man of monumental pettiness and eccentricity, with a hundred categories of hatreds and dislikes." What, I wonder, is the source of this description, written in 1970? Bernard Sobel was the press agent of the *Ziegfeld Follies* for ten years. He covered most of Fields' appearances in that show, including his last, in 1925. At that time, Fields was a man of forty-six, completely formed as a comedian, completely set as a private person. Sobel, in his book *Broadway Heartbeat* (1953), writing about Fields' distorted biographies, says, "Hollywood made him an autocrat whose odd behavior was matched only by his drinking prowess. Somehow, I can't believe that Fields let fame distort him."

No, it wasn't fame that distorted Fields. It was sickness and the clutching fear of being discarded to die on the Hollywood rubbish heap. If he must play a nasty old drunk and be publicized as a nasty old drunk in order to work on the Edgar Bergen radio show, then so be it. He was an isolated person. As a young man, he stretched out his hand to Beauty and Love and they thrust it away. Gradually he reduced reality to exclude all but his work, filling the gaps with alcohol whose dim eyes transformed the world into a distant view of harmless shadows. He was also a solitary person. Years of traveling alone around the world with his juggling act taught him the value of solitude and the release it gave his mind. He abhorred bars, nightclubs, parties, and other people's houses. He seems to have left no diaries, no letters, no serious autobiographical material. Most of his life will remain unknown. But, as Ruskin said, the history of no life is a jest.

The tragedy of film history is that it is fabricated, falsified, by the very people who make film history. It is understandable that in the early years of film production, when nobody believed there was going to be any film history, most film magazines and books printed trash, aimed only at fulfilling the public's wish to share a fairy-tale existence with its movie idols. But since about 1950 film has been established as an art, and its history recognized as a serious matter. Yet film celebrities continue to cast themselves as stock types—nice or naughty girls, good or bad boys—whom their chroniclers spray with a shower of anecdotes.

The most heartbreaking of all these books is Mack Sennett's *King of Comedy* (1954), taped and written by Cameron Shipp. Except in superficial observations, Sennett had not faith enough in his genius to risk a serious, luminous exposition of his world of comedy and the immortal grotesques who inhabited it. This world of universal laughter was silenced by its exclusion when the film corporations lengthened their feature films and filled out programs with animated cartoons and newsreels. As a part of film history, as a person who was *there*, Sennett might have given readers the truth about the mysteriously manipulated scandals that destroyed two of his greatest stars—Mabel Normand and Fatty Arbuckle. But he so abused dates and facts that, for the most part, his anecdotes are historically worthless. What he had to say about Fields' salary and drinking habits is simply a footnote to his own vanity. Only one line in his book reminds me of the Mack Sennett I used to see in the Hollywood Roosevelt Hotel when I was living there, in 1936. Almost every day, from about noon, he would sit in the lobby for a couple of hours, smoking his cigars, watching the people go by. He was then only fifty-one—a big, healthy, wonderfully handsome and virile man. How could *he* have allowed himself to be discarded to die on the Hollywood rubbish heap? Although he spoke to no one, he was never bored. As he followed with keen and unembarrassed attention my flights in and out of the hotel, I wondered what thoughts lay behind the expressionless mask he wore in public. Now I know he was practicing the art of paying attention. In his book, speaking of working for D. W. Griffith in New York, he says, "I learned all I ever learned about making pictures by standing around watching people who knew how." Anyone who has achieved excellence in any form knows that it comes as a result of ceaseless concentration. Paying attention.

I was in the *Ziegfeld Follies* with W. C. Fields in 1925. When I was eighteen, I cabled Otto Kahn, the New York banker, begging him to rescue me from London, where I was dancing the Charleston at the Café de Paris. He cabled Edmund Goulding, the future film director, who was visiting his family in London, telling Goulding to pay my rent at 49A Pall Mall and deposit me on the S.S. *Homeric* sailing for New York on February 14. Upon my arrival there, Flo Ziegfeld, who had been looking for me ever since I disappeared from the chorus of *George White's Scandals*, in September, 1924, gave me a job in the musical comedy *Louie the 14th*, starring Leon Errol. It opened at William Randolph Hearst's Cosmopolitan Theatre in March, 1925. The stage director of *Louie* was the Englishman Teddy Royce. He was an elfin creature with snapping black eyes, who whisked about on the coldest winter days dressed only in a tweed suit with a gray cashmere scarf wound around his neck. (He died in England in 1965, at the age of ninety-four.) He detested all of Ziegfeld's spoiled beauties, but most of all me, because on occasion, when I had other commitments, I would wire to the theatre notice of my nonappearance. (In May, at Famous Players-Lasky's studio, in New York, under Herbert Brenon's direction, I had played with no enthusiasm a bit part in *Street of Forgotten Men.*) One day in June, Teddy Royce called the girls together onstage after the Wednesday matinée. I came on last, standing inconspicuously at the end of the line onstage right. Centered behind the orchestra pit stood Mr. Royce, sipping his gin and water. After some vague remarks about the lack of discipline in the theatre, he looked sharply at me and said, "Some girls in this show are using the theatre exclusively as a showcase." All the girls looked at me, too, and grinned happily. I was humiliated and insulted. I rushed to the little den under the stage box, which Mr. Ziegfeld used for consultations, and told him how Mr. Royce had publicly humiliated and insulted me. He smiled his charming, silver-fox smile and instantly transferred me to the *Follies.*

When I arrived backstage at the New Amsterdam Theatre to start rehearsals for the summer edition of the *Follies,* I asked Billy Shrode, the stage manager, for the number of my dressing room. He looked at my makeup box, looked at the callboard, upon which was posted a list of dressing rooms and their occupants, then looked at me. "To tell you the truth, Louise," he said, laughing in spite of himself, "I've asked them all and there's not a girl in the show willing to dress with you."

Having won no popularity contests with the girls in the *Scandals* and *Louie the 14th,* I received this news without comment.

"What the devil do you do to these girls?" Shrode asked.

"I don't do *anything* to them."

"Maybe that's it," he said, and, shaking his head, turned back to the dressing-room list.

The fierce status battles over theatre dressing rooms have sometimes driven stars from shows, and even closed them. The dressing-room situation in the New Amsterdam was peculiar, because that theatre was the only one in New York then allowed by fire laws to be sheathed in an office building. Offstage on the ground floor was a single star dressing room. Because Will Rogers came to the theatre wearing his cowboy outfit, carrying his lasso, and chewing his gum, ready to go onstage for his monologue, there was no problem about giving the star dressing room to W. C. Fields. Breaking all the other rules of protocol, Ziegfeld devoted the second floor to his showgirls—the tall girls who did not dance but merely paraded across the stage in elaborate costumes—who, in case they missed the elevator, must not exhaust themselves walking down more than a single flight of stairs to the stage. The principals dressed on the third floor, the chorus girls—the shorter girls, who did dance—on the fourth. On the fifth floor was another single dressing room, a duplicate of the star's. Dorothy Knapp, Ziegfeld's most glorified beauty, dressed here alone. It was decided that I should share her glory.

We were a harmonious couple. Between Dorothy and me there was neither jealousy nor competition. For Dorothy, it was not enough to walk across the stage dressed in little except her breathless beauty. Although her screen tests had been unsuccessful, she still yearned to become a movie star, and took lessons in acting and dancing toward that end. For me, who had danced with Ruth St. Denis, Ted Shawn, and Martha Graham, my little dances in the *Follies* were boring. I would rather have been a showgirl. My moment of delight came at the end of the *Follies*, when the whole company was onstage for the finale. Will Rogers and I climbed a ladder to the top of a fifteen-foot tower set in the middle of the stage. Starting with a tiny noose on his lasso, Rogers would twirl it faster and faster, bigger and bigger, until the rope hissed in a circle around us like an intoxicated snake as the curtains opened and the dazzling spotlight shone upon us.

The fifth-floor dressing room lost its exclusive atmosphere when the chorus girl Peggy Fears, who had also transferred from *Louie* to the *Follies*, decided to become my best friend. She was a darling girl, with a sweet singing voice, from Dallas. She had smooth, chestnut-colored hair, untouched by dyes or permanent waves. Instead of the expensive offstage gowns of a *Follies* girl, she wore schoolgirl sweaters and skirts. Perhaps it was her whimsical sense of fun that attracted her to me. For what could be more fun than for Peggy, the most popular girl in the show, to become friends with its most abominated member —me? One night, she crashed our dressing room carrying a Wedgwood teapot full of corn whiskey and, knowing my literary pretensions, two disgustingly vulgar magazines—*Broadway Brevities* and *The Police Gazette*. A week later, we were living together in the Gladstone Hotel, off Park Avenue, where Peggy's friends swarmed until September, when she went on tour with the *Follies* and I went into *The American Venus* at Famous Players-Lasky's Long Island studio.

It was through Peggy Fears that I came to know Bill Fields. At the Rosary Florist, on Park Avenue, before the matinée, she would select a bouquet to be wrapped in waxed paper and presented to Bill in his dressing room. It touched his heart. Bill adored beautiful girls, but few were invited to his dressing room. He was morbidly sensitive about the eczema that inflamed his nose and sometimes erupted on his hands, so that he had had to learn to juggle wearing gloves. After several devastating experiences with beautiful girls, he had decided to restrict himself to girlfriends who were less attractive, and whom he would not find adrift with saxophone players. Bill repeatedly entertained Peggy and me with distinction. His bar was an open wardrobe trunk, fitted with shelves, which was planted, as if it were an objet d'art, beside his chair. While Shorty, the silent dwarf who was his valet and his assistant onstage, went about preparing our drinks, Peggy and I would dance around Bill, who sat at his makeup shelf listening to our nonsense with gracious attention.

I have never loved and laughed at W. C. Fields in films as I loved and laughed at him in the theatre. There are three reasons. First, in the theatre, he was a make-believe character playing in a make-believe world. In films, he was a real character acting in real stories. On the stage, the crafty idiocy with which he attempted to extricate himself from ludicrous situations was unbelievably funny. The same idiocy attending the same situations on the screen gave his "real" character sometimes a degraded quality, often a cruel and destructive one.

Every night at the *Follies*, standing in the wings, I would watch Bill's "Bedroom Sketch," with Edna Leedom, and his "Picnic Sketch," with Ray Dooley. The "Bedroom Sketch" opens in darkness. Bill and Edna are asleep in a double bed facing the audience. On Bill's side is a night table with a lamp on it; on Edna's side is a night table with a telephone on it. The telephone rings. Bill turns on the lamp and gets out of bed, sodden with sleep, his hair on end, wearing rumpled old white pajamas. He trots round the bed on his little pink feet to answer the telephone. After mumbling a few words, he says, "Good night, Elmer." Then, looking down at Edna, who neither moves nor speaks, he adds, "That was Elmer." Bill turns out the light and gets back into bed. The telephone rings again. This time, when Bill says, "That was Elmer," Edna sits up in a fury. She is lovely. Her blond hair is in perfect order and her lace nightgown exposes her lovely bosom and arms. Her anger does not hide the merriment in her eyes and the dimples in her cheeks. While they fight over the identity of Elmer, nobody in the audience is expected to believe that Edna is Bill's jealous wife. The film *International House* (1933) contains a bedroom sequence played by Bill in the same old white pajamas, with another lovely blonde in an exquisite nightgown—Peggy Hopkins Joyce. But the realistic distaste with which she regards Bill spoils the fun.

In the *Follies*, Bill, as a father, played the "Picnic Sketch" with Ray Dooley as his small daughter. At that time, Ray, although she was twenty-eight, with two children of her own, had the face of an infant monkey and a body that fitted nicely into a baby carriage. Her portrayals of obnoxious kids, aged from two to six, were brilliant travesties. She was not the aggressive child usual in theatre sketches. Up to the moment of an outburst, she was a passive child, following Bill's operations, her eyes glazed with anxiety. Making no sound, she watched him break in the door of an unoccupied house upon whose lawn was to be spread the litter of the picnic lunch. He burst into the house, outraged to find the door locked against honest, taxpaying Americans, and came out in triumph with a paper bag filled with stolen food. It was only after he opened a can of tomatoes with a hatchet, squirting the red juice in his face, that she set up the howls that made him flinch and recoil and yank his straw hat over his ears. As the traditional obnoxious kid, a little boy, Mickey Bennett, played Ray Dooley's part in the same picnic sequence in the film *It's the Old Army Game* (1926), in which I played the love interest. It was shot on the front lawn of the most lavish estate in Palm Beach—El Mirasol, the winter home of a J. P. Morgan partner, Edward Stotesbury. Not only was it a most improbable spot for a Fields picnic but what the production unit did to the lawn was frightful. During five days of shooting, the litter converted it into a garbage dump; and when the trucks and forty pairs of feet finished their work, it looked like the abandoned site of an old soldiers' reunion.

My second reason for preferring Fields on the stage to Fields on the screen is that on the stage the audience saw all of him all the time. In 1925, when we were both working at Famous Players-Lasky's Long Island studio, I in *The American Venus* and he in *Sally of the Sawdust*, I would go to his set to watch him work. He paid no attention to camera setups. For each shot, he would rehearse the same business to exasperating perfection while his co-star, Carol Dempster, and the director D. W. Griffith sat bored and limp in chairs beside the camera. Long shot, medium shot, two-shot, or closeup, Bill performed as if he were standing whole before an audience that could appreciate every detail of his costume and follow the dainty disposition of his hands and feet. Every time the camera drew closer, it cut off another piece of him and deprived him of some comic effect.

Having thousands of feet of close shots at his disposal, the film editor supplies my third reason for loving the stage Fields more than the film Fields. Fields never really left the theatre. As he ignored camera setups, he ignored the cutting room, and he could only curse the finished film, seeing his timing ruined by haphazard cuts.

William LeBaron, head of the New York Paramount Studio, was responsible for attempting to divert Fields from fantasy to realism. Today, it is assumed that Fields was a big box-office star in the theatre and in films. He was not. The largest audience he attracted was the radio audience of 1937–38, which listened to his unedited dialogue with another creature of the imagination, Edgar Bergen's dummy Charlie McCarthy. But back in 1925 LeBaron believed that Fields could never achieve complete success without becoming a real person to the audience. Producing Marion Davies' films for Hearst, LeBaron had almost brought Marion to life in *When Knighthood Was in Flower* (1922). With *Little Old New York* (1923), he produced her first hit, in which, dressed in boys' clothes, she acted like a real girl. After seeing Fields successfully play a character part in *Poppy*, LeBaron gave him a part in Marion's film *Janice Meredith* (1924). When LeBaron moved to Paramount, he put Fields under contract. Between 1925 and 1938, LeBaron produced twenty-one Fields films. Yet it was after Fields escaped realism and returned to his world of make-believe that he made his best films. These were produced at Universal, between 1938 and 1941. This is a puzzling fact, considering that it was LeBaron who produced all the exhilarant Mae West fantasies at Paramount, managing to neutralize her schemes to portray a *real* femme fatale—or, as Fields put it, "a plumber's idea of Cleopatra."

The first of five Fields films directed by Eddie Sutherland was *It's the Old Army Game.* To shoot exteriors in February, 1926, Paramount sent the production unit to Ocala, an inland farming town in Florida. About six miles away was Silver Springs, which was advertised as having "one hundred and fifty natural springs issuing from the porous Ocala limestone and flowing into a common basin." The basin was filled with tropical fish, surrounded by tropical plants and flowers. This iridescent beauty was viewed from a glass-bottomed motorboat, which Eddie used for a love scene between William

Gaxton and me. The citizens of Ocala, hoping to make Silver Springs a rich tourist attraction, welcomed our company as a means of publicizing their project. We were treated to so much Southern hospitality that the script got lost and the shooting schedule wandered out of sight. Nobody in Ocala seemed to have heard of Prohibition. And if ever there was a company that needed no help in the consumption of liquor it was ours. Eddie and Tom Geraghty (the writer) drank; William Gaxton, Blanche Ring, the crew, and I—everyone drank. Bill Fields, apart, drank his private stock with his girlfriend, Bessie Poole; his manager, Billy Grady; and his valet, Shorty. We were a week over schedule, and LeBaron was wiring to us "All second cameraman's rushes tilted. What are you doing? Sober up and come home," when Eddie decided that the picnic sequence absolutely must be shot on Mrs. Stotesbury's lawn.

Palm Beach was especially attractive that year, because its millionaires had decided that they could not get through the winter without their *Follies* girls. They had provided Ziegfeld with the money to produce *Palm Beach Nights*, a small edition of the *Follies*. It was housed in an old assembly hall transformed by the famous Viennese designer Joseph Urban into a nightclub with a full stage. Ziegfeld provided a choice selection of *Follies* girls, including Paulette Goddard, who later married Charlie Chaplin, and Susan Flemming, who later married Harpo Marx. And now every night, at the conclusion of *Palm Beach Nights*, our company (minus Bill Fields) contributed a floor show. Blanche Ring sang "Rings on My Fingers," Mickey Bennett sang ballads in a piercing tenor, I danced, Eddie did pratfalls, and Billy Gaxton starred as a comedian. He and Rudy Cameron did an old vaudeville act of theirs, singing and dancing and telling bum jokes with violent self-approval. Then Gaxton appeared alone, playing the violin. This was even worse than the vaudeville act. Trying to recapture the essence of Gaxton's impromptu comedy, I realize now that it was born of despair, because he was funny every day, too. When we did not work, he was funny reading *Gentlemen Prefer Blondes* to me; when we worked, he was funny about his makeup, always checking with the cameraman, Alvin Wyckoff, to see whether a scar on the back of his neck was well covered, since it was the only part of him that showed in our two-shots together. I knew that our parts as the "love interest" in a Fields comedy meant nothing, but Gaxton had convinced himself that this first job in films would launch him on a successful new career, allowing him to escape from years of mediocre vaudeville sketches. At best, it was a mistaken act of friendship—Eddie's giving the part of a boy to a sophisticated actor of thirty-four. Billy Gaxton was so vulnerable, so proud of his good looks, his Spanish ancestry, his acting ability. When he became a great Broadway star in George Gershwin's *Of Thee I Sing* (1931), the deadly bitterness of what he regarded as his failure in *It's the Old Army Game* was exposed by the fact that he refused fantastic contracts, and never made another film.

Not having seen *It's the Old Army Game*, I know only that it did not make money. In 1927, when Eddie directed his second Fields comedy, a remake of Mack Sennett's *Tillie's Punctured Romance*, Paramount's Long Island studio was closed, LeBaron had left Paramount, and Fields was finishing his contract at the Hollywood studio. I was still married to Eddie during the preparation and production of *Tillie*, which was the worst mess of filmmaking that I have ever observed. Even Fields, who ordinarily had nothing to do with a picture until shooting began, came to our house one afternoon to look into the story, which was told to him by Eddie and the writer, Monte Brice. I remember Bill sitting quietly, listening and drinking martinis from Eddie's two-quart cocktail shaker; I remember him teasing me by dropping my fragile Venetian wineglasses and catching them just before they hit the floor; but I can't remember one word he said about the idiotic plot contrived for the remake of the film.

Mack Sennett's *Tillie's Punctured Romance* had been a box-office hit in 1914, owing to the presence of Charlie Chaplin and Mabel Normand. The title and the story had no value in 1927, when Paramount (which had bought all of Sennett's properties) sold the rights, along with the services of Fields and Sutherland, to Al and Charlie Christie. The Christie brothers had been making the popular Christie Comedies since 1916. They were kind, big men, nearing fifty when the large film corporations established the controlling theatre chains that eliminated the Christies' two-reel comedies, as they eliminated Sennett's. Temporary insanity brought on by the prospect of losing their company, their studio, and their Beverly Hills mansion induced the Christies to produce the six-reel *Tillie* with a Paramount release. It was filmed with groans, previewed with moans, shown in a few theatres, and then buried in the vaults. Poor old *Tillie* had not a single mourner.

After a famous person dies, his biographers feel free to give him a glittering list of intimate friends. Anecdotes are so much tastier spiced with expensive names. Bill Fields' list grows with every telling. As far as I know, he had no intimate friends, and he loved only one person, whose name, Paul Jones, is meaningless to practically everyone. Paul Meredith Jones was born in 1897, in Bristol, Tennessee, a mountain village on the Kentucky border. In 1922, he turned up at the Paramount studio and got a job as a prop boy. In 1962, when he retired from that studio, he left behind one of the finest records as a comedy producer known to Hollywood history. He had produced comedies with Bing Crosby and Bob Hope; with Hope alone; with Martin and Lewis; with Jerry Lewis alone; with Danny Kaye; and with W. C. Fields. In 1931, while Paul was still an assistant director, LeBaron returned to Paramount and began to groom him as a comedy producer. Although LeBaron was tall and gray and elegant, and Paul was a small, sandy-haired hillbilly, they had much in common. Both were serene, witty observers of the scene rather than participants— warm and friendly, yet remote. Both were unpublicized, unknown in Hollywood society. But whereas LeBaron functioned above the storm, he could send Paul to any set where insecure comedians were fighting with insecure comedy directors, and obtain peace.

Fields, Eddie, and I first knew Paul when he was the second assistant on *It's the Old Army Game*. His walk alone—the way he came on the set, as if he had ambled down the mountain to make a friendly call—was as soothing as a lullaby. Leaning on his cane, as relaxed as if he were leaning over a rail fence, his narrow eyes twinkling in his long, solemn face, he would listen to Bill and Eddie argue about the direction of a scene until they ran out of words. Then, with some easy, comforting remarks, he would make them feel just silly enough to laugh at themselves. When it came time to shoot the scene, the argument had settled itself—usually in Bill's favor. Paul became first assistant on *Tillie's Punctured Romance*. That is when he became Fields' confidant. They had a bond: women. Paul, too, adored beautiful girls who did not adore him. His handicap was his total distinctiveness. He did not look or act or talk like anyone else in Hollywood. Young girls were ashamed to go out with "that little hillbilly." He had fallen in love with a pretty extra girl, Doris Hill, and persuaded Eddie to give her a part in *Tillie*. During production, she met Monte Brice and married him.

The last time I saw Paul was in 1940, at his home. He had become a powerful and wealthy producer without changing a bit. He was married to his pleasant secretary, Julia, and they were living in an old-fashioned bungalow on an unfashionable street in Hollywood. I was soon to leave Hollywood forever, and Paul's stories and imitations of Bill Fields are the last happy memories I possess of that unhappy place. Especially Bill's plot to get rid of Bessie Poole. Bessie was a large, plump blonde who wore ruffled pink organdy dresses with matching hat, gloves, shoes, and parasol. Her composure was indestructible. All Bill's suggestions that she should leave him for her own good were deflected with smiling contentment. Not being a cruel man or a brave one, he designed a painless separation by means of a fictional business trip, taking Paul with him to San Francisco. Bessie saw them off in Hollywood, waving goodbye, with her pink handkerchief, to Bill and Paul, who were standing on the observation platform of the train. All the time Bill was waving and beaming and calling goodbye to Bessie, he was muttering his horrid plot into Paul's ear. When they arrived in San Francisco, he would telephone his lawyer in Hollywood, instructing him to present a generous check to Bessie and then stuff her on the first train back to New York and the burlesque show she had come from. Paul knew, of course, that Fields would never have the courage to carry out the plot, which seemed so feasible as the train was pulling out and he was calling, "Goodbye, Bessie! Goodbye, my dear—my little rosebud! Take care of yourself!"

SIX | *Gish and Garbo*

There was a time when I had a great deal to say about the failure of the most powerful film stars to maintain the quality of uniqueness which had first made them the idols of the public. I found a great deal to condemn in their lack of judgment in accepting poor pictures. In the spring of 1958, looking at Lillian Gish in *One Romantic Night* (an adaptation of Molnár's *The Swan*), I could not understand how she could have gone back to Hollywood in 1929 to play that ghostly part in that foolish picture made in the place from which, two years before, her spirit had gone forever—"forgotten by the place where it grew." But now, after penetrating more deeply into the picture executives' aims and methods, I can only wonder and rejoice at the power of personality, intellect, and will that kept Lillian Gish a star for fifteen years. I can only be endlessly grateful that she was able to make so many marvelous pictures before the producers found the trick of curbing a star and standardizing their product according to their own will and personal taste.

Old pictures were bad pictures. Pictures were better than ever. An actor was only as good as his last picture. These three articles of faith were laid down by the producers, and business was conducted in a manner to prove them. As for the public, it was taught to sneer at old pictures. People had been accustomed to seeing the same things over and over and loving them more and more—the same minstrel shows and vaudeville acts, the same Sothern and Marlowe in *The Merchant of Venice*. Why not the same Lon Chaney in *The Hunchback of Notre Dame*? Or the same Pola Negri in *Passion*? But Hollywood feared and believed without question that what it said was true. Even Charlie Chaplin believed—he whose supreme success depended chiefly on the continued showing of his old pictures. Among all the creative minds of the picture business, D. W. Griffith alone knew the lie. "The public isn't fickle about its stars," he said in 1926. "Stars do not slip quickly, despite the theory to the contrary. You hear that So-and-So will die if he doesn't get a good picture immediately. Consider how many weak pictures have been made by big favorites—who are still favorites." But who cared what Griffith said?

The year 1925 was when two things happened that finally bound the producers together in a concerted war on the star system. First, 1925 was the terrible year when the industry suddenly found itself in subjection to Wall Street. Modestly declaring a hands-off policy up to then, the bankers had been financing the producers in their effort to buy up the country's 20,500 picture theatres and had been encouraging them to spend $250 million a year on theatre construction. But now bankers were sitting in on board meetings and giving producers orders. Bankers, having penetrated the secrets of the picture corporations' books and discovered the studio overhead (a sum of money executives added to a film budget to later split among themselves), were receiving generous shares of the once private "golden harvest" of the producers. Then, finding that it wasn't the name of a lion roaring on a title sheet but the name of a star which drew a multi-million-dollar gross at the box office, bankers were beginning to object to the abuse of stars. Naturally, the producers did not so much as consider giving up the practice of cutting salaries and firing stars— their customary way of making up their losses and refreshing their prestige. The solution was simply to use a subtler technique, to be confirmed by box-office failure. Marked first for destruction was Lillian Gish. She was the obvious choice. Of all the detestable stars who stood between the movie moguls and the full realization of their greed and self-aggrandizement, it was Lillian Gish who most painfully imposed her picture knowledge and business acumen upon the producers. She was a timely martyr as well, being Hollywood's radiant symbol of purity standing in the light of the new sex star.

The year 1925 was also the year when Will Hays succeeded in killing censorship in twenty-four states. Of these, New York was the only one that mattered —meaning New York City, where Mr. Hays had thoughtfully set up the National Board of Review. The Board was "opposed to legal censorship and in favor of the constructive method of selecting the better pictures," and had already put a passing mark on the producers' test runs of adult pictures of sexual realism: *A Woman of Paris, Greed,* and *The Salvation Hunters.* These pictures had been tolerated by the public, too. It had accepted the new hero, with the conscienceless sophistication of Adolphe Menjou and the unbridled manliness of John Gilbert—an acceptance based on the beloved proposition that practically all women are whores anyway. Everything was set for the collection of the treasure at the box office, where the producers' hearts lay, when they were pulled up short by the realization that they had no heroine with youth, beauty, and personality enough to make free love sympathetic. To be seen as beautifully handled, a female star's picture still had to have a tag showing marriage. Mae Murray, fighting for her virtue against von Stroheim's direction in *The Merry Widow,* had proved the impossibility of transmuting established stars into the new gold. The worldly-woman type, given a whirl with Edna Purviance, Florence Vidor, and Aileen Pringle, was too remote and mature to interest the public. The passionate Pola Negri, after being worked over by Paramount for three years, was dead at the box office. And the producers were driving actresses out of their minds—draping Barbara LaMarr in a nun's veil to make her sympathetic, and sticking a rose between the teeth of Hollywood's most celebrated screen virgin, Lois Wilson, to make her sexy. And then, in the early spring of 1925, Louis B. Mayer found her! Looking at Greta Garbo in the Swedish picture *Gösta Berling*, in Berlin, he knew as sure as he was alive that he had found a sexual symbol beyond his or anyone else's imagining. Here was a face as purely beautiful as Michelangelo's Mary of the *Pietà*, yet glowing with passion. The suffering of her soul was such that the American public would forgive her many affairs in *The Torrent*, Garbo's first American picture. At last, marriage—the obstacle standing between sex and pleasure—could be done away with! At last, here was an answer to young actresses who wanted to play good girls!

As for the established women stars, it was only a question of a year or two before the powerful support of the studios would be withdrawn from all of them. The timely coincidence of the advent of talking pictures provided a plausible reason to give the public for the disappearance of many favorites. But there wasn't an actress in Hollywood who didn't understand the true reason. Greta Garbo. From the moment *The Torrent* went into production, no contemporary actress was ever again to be quite happy in herself. The whole M-G-M studio, including Monta Bell, the director, watched the daily rushes with amazement as Garbo created out of the stalest, thinnest material the complex, enchanting shadow of a soul upon the screen. And it was such a gigantic shadow that people didn't speak of it. At parties, two or three times a week, I would see Norma Shearer and Irving Thalberg, Hunt Stromberg, Paul Bern, Jack Conway, and Clarence Brown, all of whom worked at M-G-M. If, by chance, one of the men was so inhumane as to speak of a Garbo picture, one of the girls would say, "Yes, isn't she divine?" and hurry on to a subject that created less despair.

A name that was never mentioned in the endless shoptalk was that of Lillian Gish. The suspicion that M-G-M had put her under contract at a spectacular salary in order methodically to destroy her might not have been forced upon me had I not seen *The Wind* at the Dryden Theatre in Rochester's Eastman House one night in 1956. I had never heard of it! And I could find no clue to its history. Gish's clothes were charmingly contrived from all periods, from no period. Her hair was either piled up in a dateless fashion on top of her head or swirling round her throat and shoulders. The Swedish director Victor Seastrom (born Sjöström), in his direction, shared her art of escaping time and place. Seastrom and Gish were meant for each other. After the picture, I could hardly wait to ask the curator of Eastman House, James Card, when and where it was made. He said that it had been made at M-G-M, in Hollywood, in 1927. "In Hollywood, in 1927, at M-G-M?" I said. "Why, I was there then, working at Paramount! How come I never heard a word about *The Wind*?" Determined to solve the mystery of its obliteration, I went at once to the files of the magazine *Photoplay*. I was aware that its editor, James Quirk, had seemed to weep and rage, dance and exult, with every heartbeat of the M-G-M executives. And I found that the last kindness *Photoplay* showed Lillian Gish, until after she left the M-G-M studio, appeared in a caption under her photograph in the October, 1924, issue. *Romola* was "one of the highly promising things of the new film season." From then on, I traced Quirk's fascinating operations on Gish as if I were Sherlock Holmes.

News of her unprecedented contract—eight hundred thousand dollars for six pictures in two years—was belatedly tossed off on a back page in June, 1925. In September, even before the first of these pictures, *La Boheme*, had gone into production, *Photoplay* became unaccountably worked up in an editorial:

What does the future hold for Lillian Gish? Criticism has its fads and fancies and it has in the past few years become fashionable to laud her as the Duse of the screen, yet, since she left Mr. Griffith's studios, nothing has appeared which should give her artistic preference over other actresses who have earned high places. She has always played the frail girl caught in the cruel maelstrom of life, battling helplessly for her honor or her happiness. She has a philosophy of life which she adheres to with a deliberateness that amounts almost to a religion, reminding me [Quirk] of a girlish "Whistler's mother." While she may not be the intellectual personality some writers are so fond of seeing in her because of her serenity, she has a soundness of business judgment which has enabled her to capitalize her screen personality with one of the largest salaries. . . . Wouldn't it be interesting to see Gish play a Barbara LaMarr role, for Duse was a versatile actress, if ever there was one?

With the release of *La Boheme*, in March, 1926, Quirk put the question to his more than two million readers in a long piece, "The Enigma of the Screen."

Lillian Gish has never become definitely established in a place of public favor. She achieves greatness of effect through a single phase of emotion —namely hysteria. . . . As a regular commercial routine star grinding on schedule with whatever material is at hand, her fate at the box-office would be as tragic as it invariably is on the screen. . . . Witnesses of the playing of scenes in *La Boheme* felt this strongly. The acting methods of John Gilbert and Miss Gish are entirely different. He expressed the opinion that she was the great artist of the screen and that she knew more *technically* than anyone else. Yet plainly his work was suffering under that method.

A "Brief Review" of *La Boheme* in the June, 1926, *Photoplay* read, "A simple love story wonderfully directed by King Vidor and acted with much skill by John Gilbert. Lillian Gish is also in the cast." In October, *The Scarlet Letter* was reviewed, with "Lillian Gish wears the red letter of sin with her stock virginal sweetness." The gossip pages were seeded with items like "Who is your choice for Lorelei Lee in *Gentlemen Prefer Blondes*? Ours is Lillian Gish. But, failing to get Lillian, we suggest that Paramount borrow the services of Harry Langdon."

With Gish, it was a question of how to get her to make a real stinker. Under her supervision, *La Boheme* and *The Scarlet Letter* were fine pictures. So when she was called away to bring her sick mother home from London, the studio carefully framed a picture postcard called *Annie Laurie*, which she returned to find all ready to shoot—sets, costumes, and the actor Norman Kerry. Back in charge, she next made *The Wind*, which was so loaded with sex and violence that M-G-M held up its release until the first Academy Award had been safely dealt to Janet Gaynor. And then Gish's strength failed, and she accepted a dreary studio property, *The Enemy*. She could go now, M-G-M said; she needn't make the sixth picture. At last, Quirk was able to set her up as an example and a warning to any actress who might presume beyond sex and beauty. M-G-M had let her go because she got eight thousand dollars a week! And, without a blush, he developed the idea that all the pictures made on her say-so were box-office failures. Stigmatized at the age of thirty-one as a grasping, silly, sexless antique, the great Lillian Gish left Hollywood forever, but not a head turned to mark her departure. "A shadow's shadow—a world of shadows."

It seems fateful now to remember that after Gish saw a screening of *Gösta Berling* she said that she had faith in L. B. Mayer because he had brought over Greta Garbo. Not possibly could she have guessed that this event would make Gish roles obsolete as fast as the studio could clean up her contract. Before production on *The Torrent* started, the studio kept Garbo hanging around the lot making publicity stills, and she was able to observe Gish at work on *La Boheme*. Watching the only American star whose integrity, dedication, and will brought her work up to the standards of order and excellence that Garbo had learned in Europe, she saw that the helpless actress being churned in a clabber of expedience, irresolution, unpredictable hours, and horseplay was not necessarily the law of American film production. The May, 1926, *Photoplay* quoted Garbo as saying, "I vill be glad when I am a beeg star like Lillian Gish. Then I vill not need publicity and to have peectures taken shaking hands with a prize fighter." *La Boheme* and *The Torrent* opened on Broadway the same week in February, 1926. *La Boheme*, a great story with a great director, King Vidor, and two great stars, Lillian Gish and John Gilbert, did average business at the Embassy Theatre. Lillian Gish got four hundred thousand dollars a year. *The Torrent*, a senseless story with a fair director and Ricardo Cortez, a comic Valentino-type leading man, and an unknown actress, Garbo, did top business at the Capitol Theatre. Garbo got sixteen thousand dollars a year.

After *The Temptress*, Garbo said, "I do not want to be a silly temptress. I cannot see any sense in getting dressed up and doing nothing but tempting men in pictures," and Quirk was moved to write in his December editorial, "When you learn to speak English, gal, inquire how many beautiful and clever girls have been absolutely ruined by playing good women without ever a chance to show how bad they could be. Some actresses would give a year's salary if they could once be permitted to play a hell-raising, double-crossing censor-teaser for six reels. There are exceptions, of course. Lillian Gish continues to demonstrate that virtue can be its own reward to the tune of eight thousand bucks a week." Nevertheless, *Anna Karenina*, which had been announced in November as going into production with Lillian Gish, became *Love* with Greta Garbo. *Love* was Garbo's first picture after she had signed a new M-G-M contract in May, 1927. Quirk had laid it on the line for Garbo in the April, 1927, *Photoplay*. "Metro is said to have told Garbo that, unless she signs, she will be deported at the end of her passport time limit, in June," he wrote. As well as she knew her genius, knew that she was queen of all movie stars—then and forever—she knew that to leave her kingdom was to become a wandering, tarnished star like all the rest. She did not really want to go home. After a long hold-out over salary, she signed, for seventy-five hundred dollars a week. Her business triumph over the studio was her collecting, with stunning impact, on seven months of nationwide publicity. The studio had not reckoned on its defeat and the consequences. And the victory of one friendless girl in an alien land over the best brains of a great corporation rocked all Hollywood.

Compared to Quirk's polished mauling of Lillian Gish, M-G-M's application of the dig-your-own-grave technique was a sloppy job, and it was not to achieve a slick finish till after the death of Irving Thalberg, in 1936, when Mayer began restocking his stables with actresses closer to his heart, working on that insoluble problem of how to make a box-office star without at the same time making her unaffordable. Eased out with full approval, in the perfection of their beauty, art, and popularity, were Jeanette MacDonald, Joan Crawford, Norma Shearer, and finally Garbo herself. Sixteen years passed between the public execution of Lillian Gish and the bloodless exile of Greta Garbo. Hollywood producers were left with their babes and a backwash of old-men stars, watching the lights go out in one picture house after another across the country.

Frank Wedekind's play *Pandora's Box* opens with a prologue. Out of a circus tent steps the Animal Tamer, carrying in his left hand a whip and in his right hand a loaded revolver. "Walk in," he says to the audience. "Walk into my menagerie!" The finest job of casting that G. W. Pabst ever did was casting himself as the director, the Animal Tamer, of his film adaptation of Wedekind's "tragedy of monsters." Never a sentimental trick did this whip hand permit the actors assembled to play his beasts. The revolver he shot straight into the heart of the audience. At the time Wedekind produced *Pandora's Box*, in Berlin around the turn of the century, it was detested, condemned, and banned. It was declared to be "immoral and inartistic." If in that period when the sacred pleasures of the ruling class were comparatively private, a play exposing them had called out the dogs of law, how much more savage would be the attack upon a film faithful to Wedekind's text which was made in 1928 in Berlin, where the ruling class publicly flaunted its pleasures as a symbol of wealth and power. And since nobody truly knows what a director is doing till he is done, nobody who was connected with the film dreamed that Pabst was risking commercial failure with the story of an "immoral" prostitute who wasn't crazy about her work and was surrounded by the "inartistic" ugliness of raw bestiality. Only five years earlier, the famous Danish actress Asta Nielsen had condensed Wedekind's play into the film *Loulou*. There was no lesbianism in it, no incest. Loulou the man-eater devoured her sex victims—Dr. Goll, Schwarz, and Schön—and then dropped dead in an acute attack of indigestion. This kind of film, with Pabst improvements, was what audiences were prepared for. Set upon making their disillusionment inescapable, hoping to avoid even any duplication of the straight bob and bangs that Nielsen had worn as Loulou, Mr. Pabst tested me with my hair curled. But after seeing the test he gave up this point and left me with my shiny black helmet, except for one curled sequence on the gambling ship.

Besides daring to film Wedekind's problem of abnormal psychology—in Wedekind's own words, "this fatal destiny which is the subject of the tragedy" —besides daring to show the prostitute as the victim, Mr. Pabst went on to the final, damning immorality of making his Lulu as "sweetly innocent" as the flowers that adorned her costumes and filled the scenes of the play. "Lulu is not a real character," Wedekind said in a commentary, "but the personification of primitive sexuality who inspires evil unaware. She plays a purely passive role." In the middle of the prologue, dressed in her boy's costume of Pierrot, she is carried by a stage hand before the Animal Tamer, who tells her, "Be unaffected, and not pieced out with distorted, artificial folly/even if the critics praise you for it less wholly./And mind—all foolery and making faces/the childish simpleness of vice disgraces." This was the Lulu, when the film was released, whom the critics praised not less wholly, but not at all. "Louise Brooks cannot act," one critic wrote. "She does not suffer. She does nothing." As far as they were concerned, Pabst had fired a blank. It was I who was struck down by my failure, although he had done everything possible to protect and strengthen me against this deadly blow. He never allowed me to be publicly identified with the film after the night, during production, when we appeared as guests at the opening of an UFA film, at the Gloria Palast. As we left the theatre, and he hurried me through a crowd of hostile moviegoers, I heard a girl saying something loud and nasty. In the cab, I began pounding his knee, insisting, "What did she say? What did she say?" Finally, he translated: "That is the American girl who is playing our German Lulu!"

In the studio, Pabst, who had a special, pervasive sense that penetrated minds and walls alike, put down all overt acts of contempt. Although I never complained, he substituted another assistant for an assistant who woke me out of my dressing-room naps by beating the door and bellowing, "Fräulein Brooks! Come!" Sitting on the set day after day, my darling maid, Josifine Müller, who had worked for Asta Nielsen and thought she was the greatest actress in the world, came to love me tenderly because I was the world's worst actress. For the same reason, the great actor Fritz Kortner, who played Schön, never spoke to me at all. Using Pabst's strength, I learned to block off painful impressions. Kortner, like everybody else on the production, thought I had cast some blinding spell over Pabst which allowed me to walk through my part. To them, it was a sorry outcome of Pabst's difficult search for Lulu, about which one of his assistants, Paul Falkenberg, said in 1955, "Preparation for *Pandora's Box* was quite a saga, because Pabst couldn't find a Lulu. He wasn't satisfied with any actress at hand, and for months everybody connected with the production went around looking for a Lulu. I talked to girls on the street, on the subway, in railway stations—'Would you mind coming up to our office? I would like to present you to Mr. Pabst.' He looked all of them over dutifully and turned them all down. And eventually he picked Louise Brooks."

How Pabst determined that I was his unaffected Lulu, with the childish simpleness of vice, was part of a mysterious alliance that seemed to exist between us even before we met. He knew nothing more of me than an unimportant part he saw me play in the Howard Hawks film *A Girl in Every Port* (1928). I had never heard of him, and had no idea he had made unsuccessful negotiations to borrow me from Paramount until I was called to the front office on the option day of my contract. My salary wasn't going to be increased. B. P. Schulberg told me that I could stay on at my old salary or quit. It was the time of the switchover to talkies, and studios were taking ugly advantage of this fact to cut contract players' salaries. Refusing to take what amounted to a cut, I quit Paramount. Almost as an afterthought, Schulberg told me about the Pabst offer, which I was now free to accept. I said I would accept it, and he sent off a cable to Pabst. All this took about ten minutes, and I left Schulberg somewhat dazed by my composure and my quick decisions.

If I had not acted at once, I would have lost the part of Lulu. At that very hour in Berlin Marlene Dietrich was waiting with Pabst in his office. Pabst later said, "Dietrich was too old and too obvious—one sexy look and the picture would become a burlesque. But I gave her a deadline, and the contract was about to be signed when Paramount cabled saying I could have Louise Brooks." It must be remembered that Pabst was speaking about the pre–Josef-von-Sternberg Dietrich. She was the Dietrich of *I Kiss Your Hand, Madame*, a film in which, caparisoned variously in beads, brocade, ostrich feathers, chiffon ruffles, and white rabbit fur, she galloped from one lascivious stare to another. Years after another trick of fate had made her a top star—for Sternberg's biographer, Herman Weinberg, told me that it was only because Brigitte Helm was not available that Sternberg looked further and found Dietrich for *The Blue Angel*—she said to Travis Banton, the Paramount dress designer who transformed her spangles and feathers into glittering, shadowed beauty, "Imagine Pabst choosing Louise Brooks for Lulu when he could have had me!"

So it is that my playing of the tragic Lulu with no sense of sin remained generally unacceptable for a quarter of a century.

Not long ago, after seeing *Pandora's Box* at Eastman House, a priest said to me, "How did you feel, playing—*that girl?*"

"Feel? I felt fine! It all seemed perfectly normal to me."

Seeing him start with distaste and disbelief, and unwilling to be mistaken for one of those women who like to shock priests with sensational confessions, I went on to prove the truth of Lulu's world by telling him of my own experience in the 1925 *Ziegfeld Follies*, when my best friend was a lesbian and I knew two millionaire publishers who, much like Schön in the film, backed shows to keep themselves well supplied with Lulus. But the priest rejected my reality exactly as Berlin had rejected its reality when we made *Pandora's Box* and sex was the business of the town. At the Eden Hotel, where I lived in Berlin, the café bar was lined with the higher-priced trollops. The economy girls walked the street outside. On the corner stood the girls in boots, advertising flagellation. Actors' agents pimped for the ladies in luxury apartments in the Bavarian Quarter. Race-track touts at the Hoppegarten arranged orgies for groups of sportsmen. The nightclub Eldorado displayed an enticing line of homosexuals dressed as women. At the Maly, there was a choice of feminine or collar-and-tie lesbians. Collective lust roared unashamed at the theatre. In the revue *Chocolate Kiddies*, when Josephine Baker appeared naked except for a girdle of bananas, it was precisely as Lulu's stage entrance was described by Wedekind: "They rage there as in a menagerie when the meat appears at the cage."

Every actor has a natural animosity toward every other actor, present or absent, living or dead. Most Hollywood directors did not understand that, any more than they understood why an actor might be tempted to withhold the rapt devotion to the master which they considered essential to their position of command. When I went to Berlin to film *Pandora's Box*, what an exquisite release, what a revelation of the art of direction, was the Pabst spirit on the set! He actually encouraged actors' disposition to hate and back away from each other, and thus preserved their energy for the camera; and when actors were not in use, his ego did not command them to sit up and bark at the sight of him. The behavior of Fritz Kortner was a perfect example of how Pabst used an actor's true feelings to add depth and breadth and power to his performance. Kortner hated me. After each scene with me, he would pound off the set and go to his dressing room. Pabst himself, wearing his most private smile, would go there to coax him back for the next scene. In the role of Dr. Schön, Kortner had feelings for me (or for the character Lulu) that combined sexual passion with an equally passionate desire to destroy me. One sequence gave him an opportunity to shake me with such violence that he left ten black-and-blue fingerprints on my arms. Both he and Pabst were well pleased with that scene, because Pabst's feelings for me, like Kortner's, were not unlike those of Schön for Lulu. I think that in the two films Pabst made with me—

Pandora's Box and *Diary of a Lost Girl*—he was conducting an investigation into his relations with women, with the object of conquering any passion that interfered with his passion for his work. He was not aroused by sexual love, which he dismissed as an enervating myth. It was sexual hate that engrossed his whole being with its flaming reality.

With adroit perversity, Pabst selected Gustav Diessl to play Jack the Ripper in *Pandora's Box*, and Fritz Rasp to play the lascivious chemist's assistant in *Diary of a Lost Girl*. They were the only actors in those films whom I found beautiful and sexually alluring. There was no complexity in Pabst's direction of the Jack the Ripper scenes. He made them a tender love passage until that terrible moment when Diessl saw the knife on the edge of the table, gleaming in the candlelight. But, conceiving the seduction scenes in *Diary of a Lost Girl* as a ballet, with me (Thymiane) as the seductress, he directed them as a series of subtle, almost wordless maneuvers between an "innocent" young girl and a wary lecher. He chose Fritz Rasp not only for the restraint with which he would play a part verging on burlesque but also for his physical grace and strength. When I collapsed in his embrace, he swept me up into his arms and carried me off to bed as lightly as if I weighed no more than my silken night-gown and robe.

Unlike most directors, Pabst had no catalogue of characters, with stock emotional responses. D. W. Griffith required giggling fits from all sexually excited virgins. If Pabst had ever shot a scene showing a virgin giggling, it would have been because someone was tickling her. It was the stimulus that concerned him. If he got that right, the actor's emotional reaction would be like life itself—often strange and unsatisfactory to an audience that was used to settled acting conventions. When *Pandora's Box* was released, in 1929, film critics objected because Lulu did not suffer after the manner of Sarah Bernhardt in *Camille*. Publicity photographs taken before the filming of *Pandora's Box* show Pabst watching me with scientific intensity. Anticipating all my scenes in his films, he contrived to put me in similar situations in real life. A well-timed second visit to the set by the actress and future filmmaker Leni Riefenstahl—gabbing and laughing off in a corner with Pabst—guaranteed my look of gloomy rejection in a closeup in *Diary of a Lost Girl*. His tested knowledge of cause and effect is part of the answer to how Pabst could shoot very fast, with little rehearsal and few takes.

I revered Pabst for his truthful picture of this world of pleasure which let me play Lulu naturally. The other members of the cast were tempted to rebellion. And perhaps that was his most brilliant directorial achievement—getting a group of actors to play unsympathetic characters, whose only motivation was sexual gratification. Fritz Kortner, as Schön, wanted to be the victim. Franz Lederer, as the incestuous son Alva Schön, wanted to be adorable. Carl Goetz wanted to get laughs playing the old pimp Schigolch. Alice Roberts, the Belgian actress who played the screen's first lesbian, the Countess Geschwitz, was prepared to go no further than repression in mannish suits. Her first day's work was in the wedding sequence. She came on the set looking chic in her Paris evening dress and aristocratically self-possessed. Then Mr. Pabst began explaining the action of the scene in which she was to dance the tango with me. Suddenly, she understood that she was to touch, to embrace, to make love to another woman. Her blue eyes bulged and her hands trembled. Anticipating the moment of explosion, Mr. Pabst, who proscribed unscripted emotional outbursts, caught her arm and sped her away out of sight behind the set. A half hour later, when they returned, he was hissing soothingly to her in French and she was smiling like the star of the picture—which she was in all her scenes with me. I was just there obstructing the view. Both in two-shots and in her close-ups photographed over my shoulder, she cheated her look past me to Mr. Pabst, who was making love to her off camera. Out of the funny complexity of this design Mr. Pabst extracted his tense portrait of sterile lesbian passion, and Mme. Roberts satisfactorily preserved her reputation. At the time, her conduct struck me as silly. The fact that the public could believe an actress's private life to be like one role in one film did not come home to me till 1964, when I was visited by a French boy. Explaining why the young people in Paris loved *Pandora's Box*, he put an uneasy thought in my mind.

"You talk as if I were a lesbian in real life," I said.

"But of course!" he answered, in a way that made me laugh to realize I had been living in cinematic perversion for thirty-five years.

Pabst, a short man, broad-shouldered and thick-chested, looked heavy in repose. But in action his legs carried him on wings that matched the swiftness of his mind. He always came on the set as fresh as a March wind, going directly to the camera to check the setup, after which he turned to his cameraman, Günther Krampf, who was the only person on the film to whom he gave a complete account of the ensuing scene's action and meaning. Never conducting group discussions with his actors, he then told each actor separately what the actor must know about the scene. To Pabst, the carry-over of the acting technique of the theatre, which froze in advance every word, every move, every emotion, was death to realism in films. He wanted the shocks of life which released unpredictable emotions. Proust wrote, "Our life is at every moment before us like a stranger in the night, and which of us knows what point he will reach on the morrow?" To prevent actors from plotting every point they would reach on the morrow, Pabst never shot quite the scenes they prepared for.

On the day we shot Lulu's murder of Schön, Fritz Kortner came on the set with his death worked out to the last facial contortion—with even his blood, the chocolate syrup that would ooze from a sponge in his mouth, carefully tested for sweetness lest it surprise an unrehearsed reaction. Death scenes are dearer than life to the actor, and Kortner's, spectacularly colored with years of theatrical dying, went unquestioned during rehearsal. Pabst left it to the mechanics of each shot to alter Kortner's performance. The smoke from the firing of the revolver became of the first importance, or the exact moment when Kortner pulled my dress off my shoulder, or the photographic consistency of the chocolate syrup— all such technical irritations broke a series of prepared emotions into unhinged fragments of reality. Dialogue was set by Pabst while he watched the actors during rehearsal. In an effort to be funny, old actors and directors have spread the false belief that any clownish thing coming to mind could be said in front of the camera in silent films. They forget that the title writer had to match his work to the actors' speech. I remember late one night wandering into the Beverly Wilshire suite of Ralph Spence, a title-writer, where he sat gloomily amidst cans of film, cartons of stale Chinese food, and empty whiskey bottles. He was trying to fix up an unfunny Beery and Hatton comedy, and no comic line he invented would fit the lip action. Silent-film fans were excellent lip-readers and often complained at the box office about the cowboy cussing furiously as he tried to mount his horse. Besides, directors like Pabst used exact dialogue to isolate and intensify an emotion. When Lulu was looking down at the dead Schön, he gave me the line *"Das Blut!"* Not the murder of my husband but the sight of the blood determined the expression on my face.

In order to see things from the film director's viewpoint, one might think how difficult it is to get a true smile in a single snapshot of a person we know. Then think of a director who faces a group of strangers, all of them certain about how they want to play their parts, some of them antagonistic, all of them full of a thousand secrets of pain and humiliation which, accidentally touched upon, may defeat the director in an utterly baffling way. No director will ever admit his fear of failing to get a performance out of an actor. Some, like Eric von Stroheim, try to arouse by viciousness any violent emotion and photograph it; some fortify themselves by the use of mugging actors; some use trick photography or symbolism. But a truly great director such as G. W. Pabst holds the camera on the actors' eyes in every vital scene. He said, "The audience must see it in the actors' eyes." In his 1926 film, *Secrets of a Soul*, he sent the actor playing a psychiatrist to take a course in psychoanalysis so he could see it in his eyes. Pabst's genius lay in getting to the heart of a person, banishing fear, and releasing the clean impact of personality which jolts an audience to life.

For two weeks, while Pabst was directing *Joyless Street* (1924), everyone was screaming at him to get rid of Garbo. He heard them not. And the day came when he gained her confidence and she gave him the purest performance of her career. Far more wonderful was his handling of Alice Roberts in *Pandora's Box*. Because getting to the heart of her was to expose very little of the generosity that makes a great actress. Her husband had money in the film. She wasn't a good actress, and her fear took the form of hating Berlin, hating her part, and hating me. Any other director would have had to settle for a wooden performance. Pabst set about wooing her in French with the desires of her own soul. In the finished picture, her part is a passionately perfect portrayal of a woman caught up in the mad, hopeless pursuit of destruction among all those characters faithless to common sense. In the same picture, the old pimp is the hero of the story. He winds up in a warm place with his booze and a plum pudding. He knows what he is, what he wants, and perseveres in getting it. Lulu loses her life with the loss of her childhood, her innocent indifference to others.

That I was a dancer and Pabst essentially a choreographer in his direction came as a wonderful surprise to both of us on the first day of shooting *Pandora's Box*. The expensive English translation of the script, which I had thrown unopened on the floor by my chair, had already been retrieved by an outraged assistant and banished, to Mr. Pabst's amusement. Consequently, I did not know that Lulu was a professional dancer trained in Paris ("Gypsy, Oriental, skirt dance") or that dancing was her mode of expression ("In my despair I dance the Can-Can"). On the afternoon of that first day, Pabst said to me, "In this scene, Schigolch rehearses you in a dance number." After marking out a small space and giving me a fast tempo, he looked at me curiously. "You can make up some little steps here—can't you?" I nodded, and he walked away. It was a typical instance of his care in protecting actors against the blight of failure. If I had been able to do nothing more than the skippity-hops of Asta Nielsen, his curious look would never have been amplified to regret, although the intensity of his concern was revealed by his delight when the scene was finished. As I was leaving the set, he caught me in his arms, shaking me and laughing as if I had played a joke on him. "But you are a professional dancer!" It was the moment when he realized that his choice of me for Lulu was instinctively right. He felt as if he had created me. I was his Lulu! However, a bouquet of roses he gave me on my arrival at the railway station in Berlin was my first and last experience of the kind of deference he paid to the other actors. From that moment, I was firmly put through my tricks, with no fish thrown in for a good performance.

Four days later, I was less wonderfully surprised when he also subjected my private life to his direction. His delight in Lulu's character belonged exclusively to the film. Off the screen, my dancing days came to an end when George Marshall, with whom I had been investigating Berlin's night life till three every morning, left for Paris. On the set the next day, I had just accepted an invitation to an "Artists' Ball" when Mr. Pabst's quiet, penetrating voice sounded behind me: "Müller! Loueess does not go out anymore at night." Josifine melted away as I began to howl in protest. "But, Mr. Pabst, I have always gone out at night when I worked! I can catch up on my sleep between scenes here at the studio. I always have!" He didn't hear me because he was busy laying down the law to Josifine who thereafter, when the day's work was done, returned me to the Eden Hotel, where I was bathed, fed, and put to bed, to be called for next morning at seven. Cross and restless, I was left to fall asleep listening to the complaints of the other poor caged beasts, across Stresemannstrasse, in the Zoologischer Garten.

In the matter of my costumes for the picture, I put up a better fight, although I never won a decision. My best punches fanned the air, because Pabst had always slipped into another position. Arriving in Berlin on Sunday and starting the picture on the following Wednesday, I found he had selected my first costume, leaving me nothing to do but stand still for a final fitting. This I let pass as an expedient, never suspecting that it would be the same with every-

With my brother, Ted Brooks, in Beverly Hills, 1928.

Marion Davies. The photograph above shows
her as she looked in her first films with her own
hair, eyebrows, lashes, and mouth makeup.

William Randolph Hearst, *second from left*, with sons William, Jr., *left*, George, *second from right*, and John, *right*. Mr. Hearst would often smilingly explain that his voice was incongruously high and thin owing to a childhood illness.

With W. C. Fields in *It's the Old Army Game*, 1926.

On Florida location with future husband, Edward Sutherland, who was directing
It's the Old Army Game, 1926.

The Canary Murder Case, 1929; (*above*) with William Powell as detective Philo Vance. The canary costume came equipped with a detachable tail so I could sit down.

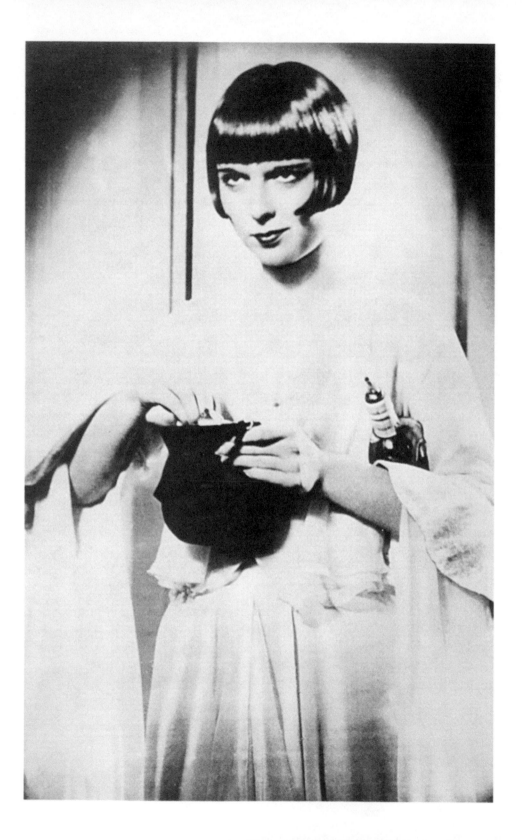

Pandora's Box, 1929; (*above*) with Fritz Kortner in
the theatre scene; (*left*) Alice Roberts refused to
play the screen's first lesbian until Pabst agreed to
"play" Lulu to her from off-camera.

OPPOSITE. The first view of Lulu, and the first scene
shot by Pabst for *Pandora's Box*.

With Kortner and Lederer in Kortner's death scene.

Fritz Kortner brutally forcing me to go on
in the theatre scene.

Moments after our wedding, Kortner
finds me in the nuptial bedroom with his son,
Franz Lederer, in my lap.

Dancing the tango with Alice Roberts as the lesbian,
to Kortner's dismay, at the wedding reception.

OPPOSITE ABOVE. With Carl Goetz, who plays the old pimp
who had seduced Lulu when she was a child.

OPPOSITE BELOW. With Kortner,
in opening sequence of *Pandora's Box*.

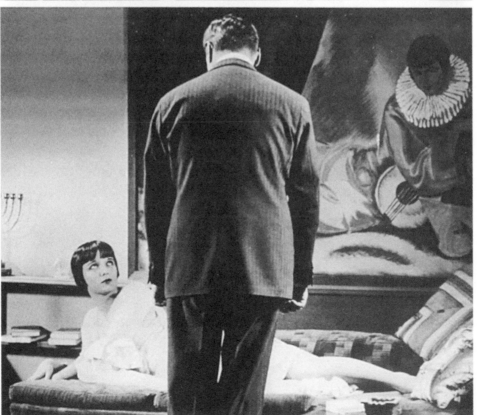

In widow's garb at the trial for Kortner's murder.

With Gustav Diessl, who played Jack the Ripper. Between shots of my death scene, the studio pianist played for me to dance the Charleston. Pabst wanted me to be innocently happy, unaware of Jack the Ripper's identity.

Diary of a Lost Girl, 1929.
With my hair combed back
in the reformatory.

With Edith Meinhard.

OPPOSITE. With Andrews
Engelmann, in *Diary*.

Diary. In the whorehouse scene (*above*) with Meinhard, *left* . . . and (*below*) with an extra in the same scene.

OPPOSITE ABOVE.
With Meinhard.

OPPOSITE BELOW.
With Fritz Rasp.

My favors being sold at auction
in *Diary*.

Drinking champagne in the whorehouse in *Diary*.

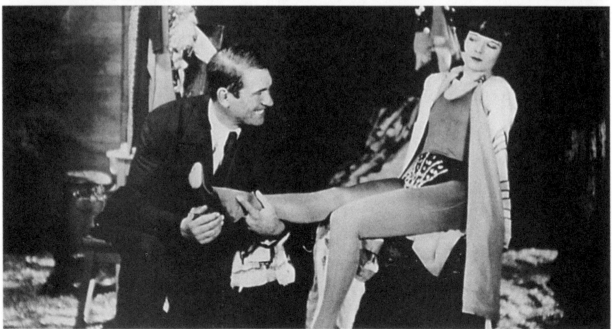

Prix de Beauté, 1930. Photographed on the set in Paris . . .
and a photograph (*above*) by Studio Lorelle, Paris.

OPPOSITE ABOVE. *God's Gift to Women*, 1931.
With Frank Fay.

OPPOSITE BELOW. *A Girl in Every Port*, 1928. With Victor McLaglen.
It was this performance that caused Pabst to cast me as Lulu
in *Pandora's Box*.

At the Fifty-ninth Street entrance to Central Park, New York, 1931, with my Pekingese, Tiki.

thing else I put on or took off, from an ermine coat to my girdle. Not only was it unheard of to allow an actress no part in choosing her clothes but I had also been spoiled by my directors at Paramount. I had played a manicurist in five-hundred-dollar beaded evening dresses; a salesgirl in three-hundred-dollar black satin afternoon dresses; and a schoolgirl in two-hundred-and-fifty-dollar tailored suits. With gross overconfidence in my rights and power, I at first defied Pabst with arrogance. Pabst chose all my costumes with care, but in scenes motivated by sexual hate he chose them as much for their tactile as for their visual seductiveness. He wanted the actors working with me to feel my flesh under a dancing costume, a blouse and skirt, a nightgown. The morning of the sequence in which I was to go from my bath into a love scene with Franz Lederer, I came on the set wrapped in a gorgeous negligee of painted yellow silk. Carrying the peignoir I refused to wear, Josifine approached Mr. Pabst to receive the lash. Hers was the responsibility for seeing that I obeyed his orders, and he answered her excuses with a stern rebuke. Then he turned to me.

"Loueess, you must wear the peignoir, and be naked under it."

"Why? I hate that bathrobe," I said. "Who will know that I am naked under that big, woolly white bathrobe?"

"Lederer," he said.

Stunned by such a reasonable argument, I retired, without another word, to the bathroom set with Josifine and changed into the peignoir.

Not to be trapped in this manner again, when I objected to the train of my wedding dress being "tied on like an apron" and he explained that it had to be easily discarded, because I could not play a long, frantic sequence tripping over my train, I answered that I did not give a damn, tore off the train, and went into an elaborate tantrum. The worst audience I ever had, Pabst instructed the dress designer to have the pieces sewn together again and left the fitting room. My final defeat, which made me cry real tears, came at the end of the picture, when he went through my trunks to select a dress to be "aged" for Lulu's murder as a streetwalker in the arms of Jack the Ripper. With his instinctive understanding of my tastes, he decided on the blouse and skirt of my very favorite suit. I was anguished. "Why can't you *buy* some cheap little dress to be ruined? Why does it have to be *my* dress?" To these questions I got no answer till the next morning, when my once lovely clothes were returned to me in the studio dressing room. They were torn and foul with grease stains. Not some indifferent rags from the wardrobe department but my own suit, which only last Sunday I had worn to lunch at the Adlon Hotel! Josifine hooked up my skirt, I slipped the blouse over my head, and I went on the set feeling as hopelessly defiled as my clothes. Working in that outfit, I didn't care what happened to me.

Dancing for two years with Ruth St. Denis and Ted Shawn had taught me much about the magic worked by authentic costuming. Their most popular duet, *Tillers of the Soil*, was costumed in potato sacking. In her *Flower Arrangement*, Miss Ruth's magnificent Japanese robes did most of the dancing. But the next three years of uncontrolled extravagance in films had so corrupted my judgment that I did not realize until I saw *Pandora's Box* in 1956 how marvelously Mr. Pabst's perfect costume sense symbolized Lulu's character and her destruction. There is not a single spot of blood on the pure-white bridal satin in which she kills her husband. Making love to her wearing the clean white peignoir, Alva asks, "Do you love me, Lulu?" "I? Never a soul!" It is in the worn and filthy garments of the streetwalker that she feels passion for the first time—comes to life so that she may die. When she picks up Jack the Ripper on the foggy London street and he tells her he has no money to pay her, she says, "Never mind. I like you." It is Christmas Eve, and she is about to receive the gift that has been her dream since childhood. Death by a sexual maniac.

It had pleased me on the day I finished the silent version of *The Canary Murder Case* for Paramount to leave Hollywood for Berlin to work for Pabst. When I got back to New York after finishing *Pandora's Box*, Paramount's New York office called to order me to get on the train at once for Hollywood. They were making *The Canary Murder Case* into a talkie and needed me for retakes. When I said I wouldn't go, they sent a man round with a contract. When I still said I wouldn't go, they offered me any amount of money I might ask, to save the great expense of reshooting and dubbing in another voice. In the end, after they were finally convinced that nothing would induce me to do the retakes, I signed a release (gratis) for all my pictures, and they dubbed in Margaret Livingston's voice in *The Canary Murder Case*. But the whole thing—the money that Paramount was forced to spend, the affront to the studio—made them so angry that they sent out a story, widely publicized and believed, that they had let me go because I was no good in talkies.

In Hollywood, I was a pretty flibbertigibbet whose charm for the executive department decreased with every increase in her fan mail. In Berlin, I stepped onto the station platform to meet Pabst and became an actress. I would be treated by him with a kind of decency and respect unknown to me in Holly-wood. It was just as if Pabst had sat in on my whole life and career and knew exactly where I needed assurance and protection. And, just as his understand-ing of me reached back to his knowledge of a past we did not have to speak about, so it was with the present. For although we were together constantly—on the set, at lunch, often for dinner and the theatre—he seldom spoke to me. Yet he would appear at the dressmaker's at the moment I was about to go into the classic act of ripping off an offensive wedding dress; he would banish a call boy who roared at me through the dressing-room door; he would refuse, after the first day's rushes, which secretly upset me, to let me see the rushes ever again. All that I thought and all his reactions seemed to pass between us in a kind of wordless communication. To other people surrounding him, he would talk endlessly in that watchful way of his, smiling, intense; speaking quietly, with his wonderful, hissing precision. But to me he might speak never a word all morning, and then at lunch turn suddenly and say, "Loueess, tomor-row morning you must be ready to do a big fight scene with Kortner," or "This afternoon, in the first scene, you are going to cry." That was how he directed me. With an intelligent actor, he would sit in exhaustive explanation; with an old ham, he would speak the language of the theatre. But in my case, by some magic, he would saturate me with one clear emotion and turn me loose. And it was the same with the plot. Pabst never strained my mind with anything not pertinent to the immediate action. But if I made that picture with only the dimmest notion of what it was about, on my second picture with Pabst, *Diary of a Lost Girl*, I had no idea at all of its plot or meaning till I saw it twenty-seven years later, at Eastman House.

And it was during the making of *Diary of a Lost Girl*—on the last day of shooting, to be exact—that Pabst moved into my future. We were sitting gloom-ily at a table in the garden of a little café, watching the workmen while they dug the grave for a burial scene, when he decided to let me have it. Several weeks before, in Paris, he had met some friends of mine—rich Americans with whom I spent every hour away from work. And he was angry: first, because he thought they prevented me from staying in Germany, learning the language, and becoming a serious actress, as he wanted; and, second, because he looked upon them as spoiled children who would amuse themselves with me for a time and then discard me like an old toy. "Your life is exactly like Lulu's," he said, "and you will end the same way."

At that time, knowing so little of what he meant by "Lulu," I just sat sullenly glaring at him, trying not to listen. Fifteen years later, in Hollywood, with all his predictions closing in on me, I heard his words again—hissing back to me. And, listening this time, I packed my trunks and went home to Kansas. But the strangest thing of all in my relationship with Mr. Pabst was the revelation tucked away in a footnote written by Richard Griffith in his book *The Film Since Then*. He identified me as "Louise Brooks, whom Pabst brought to Germany from Hollywood to play in *Pandora's Box*, whose whole life and career were altered thereby." When I read that, thirty years after I refused to go back to Hollywood to do those retakes on *The Canary Murder Case*, I finally understood why.

Epilogue

Why I Will Never Write My Memoirs

"The trouble with us," said Grant Clarke to me in 1930, "is that we are too degenerate for one part of Hollywood and not degenerate enough for the other."

This sour observation covered the fact that we were both Midwesterners born in the Bible Belt of Anglo-Saxon farmers who prayed in the parlor and practiced incest in the barn. And, although our sexual education had been conducted by the elite of Paris, London, and New York, our pleasure was restricted by the inbred shackles of sin and guilt. Thus at the same time our reputation for immorality excluded us from the parties of respectable Hollywood, which devoted itself to presenting a picture of moral beauty to the world, our reputation for sudden attacks of puritanism excluded us from the delights of the carefully arranged parties that ended for us after lunch or dinner when we were dismissed with a firm goodbye.

I am not speaking of those vulgar brawls publicized as Hollywood orgies, nor of those parties composed of a herd of extra girls infiltrated by producers and actors stimulated by stag movies, nor of those drunken parties that spread into bedrooms and out upon lawns. I am speaking of those rare entertainments which, so far as I know, have never been recorded in any memoir.

Also unrecorded in Hollywood memoirs is the name of Grant Clarke. Although his bitter witticisms are woven into film history ("Hollywood is like floating through a sewer in a glass-bottomed boat"), they are always attributed to Wilson Mizner, the famous raconteur whose gold rush stories, manufactured after five years of larceny in the Klondike, were longer than an arctic night. He held his audience with the combination of his great physical size and the command of an army general. At my house in 1927, during a repeat of the story of a miner who froze to death while stooping to tie his shoelace and had to be buried in a bass drum, as I rose to mix a cocktail Wilson circled me with his arm and set me upon his knee, imprisoned till the end of the story.

In New York in 1909, at thirty-three, he was selling gambling anecdotes to playwrights and cultivating his fame as a prize-fight manager with sportswriters when he adopted Grant Clarke, the eighteen-year-old boy wonder of lyric writers who kept Wilson in fresh jokes until his death from an overdose of morphine in Hollywood in 1931. When Wilson died in 1933 Warner Brothers was paying him to tell underworld stories to its writers at the same time he continued to collect his basic income from the gambling joints to which he steered his friends.

One night I was sitting in the Coconut Grove at the Ambassador Hotel with my truest and most adoring friend, Fred Levy, when I saw Wilson and asked him to join us. Although I detested gambling and knew nothing about it, I was so bored with Fred that I asked Wilson to take us to a gambling house. There, while Fred played twenty-one, I was entertained with champagne, perched on a stool at the dice table. Later, breakfasting at the Brown Derby with Wilson and Fred, I flourished my astonishing winnings of two hundred dollars without relating them to Fred's loss of two thousand dollars. A year after this incident, at the Chez Paris, a nightclub in Chicago, the waiter handed me a note addressed to "The come-on girl for Wilson Mizner." Looking up, I saw Fred Levy at a table across the dance floor. He waved and smiled and never saw me again.

Wilson Mizner was a creator of nothing in films. Nevertheless his fame expands yearly in film books. The obliterated Grant Clarke wrote songs still heard in films. He wrote songs for Al Jolson in *The Jazz Singer*, and for Fanny Brice he wrote her greatest song, "Second Hand Rose." The Hollywood literary code, which requires authors and publishers to substitute the names of celebrities for the lesser known names of the originators of jokes and anecdotes, increasingly distorts film history. Soon only the authors' names will distinguish one memoir from another.

The obliteration of the great director Edmund Goulding in film history returns us to sex in Hollywood.

When I was preparing to write this article I could find scarcely a trace of Edmund Goulding in my biographical notebooks. At the library, Bill Cuseo found him unlisted in *The Readers' Guide to Periodical Literature* and *The Dictionary of National Biography*. His 1959 obituary was carried only in the *New York Times* and the trade paper *Variety*. No other nationally read publication found his life and death newsworthy. This incomparable film director who was also a successful actor, singer, songwriter, novelist, playwright, and screenwriter. This incomparable human being who, when he learned in 1932 that his close friend, the English dancer Marjorie Moss, had given up her fight with tuberculosis, married her and filled the last three years of her life with beauty and the loving attendance of friends.

In June 1977 when Kevin Brownlow went to Hollywood to interview old filmmakers for the Thames TV series on silent pictures, I asked him to question them about Eddie Goulding. Two weeks later he reported that no one would talk about Goulding. His name evokes a vision of sex without sin which paralyzes the guilty mind of Hollywood. All for love he directed his sexual events with the same attention he gave the directing of films. His clients might be the British aristocracy, bankers, or corporation executives. His call girls might be waitresses or movie stars. During a thirty-eight-year career he touched the lives of many people who subsequently withdrew from his name. In 1925 after directing *Sally, Irene, and Mary*, how his blue eyes sparkled as he told Walter Wanger and me that he had discovered a new star in Joan Crawford. He taught her the fundamentals of acting, and wrote and directed *Paris* for her in 1926. Yet her numerous autobiographical writings brush him aside with a bare, necessary acknowledgment. What a contrast is Bette Davis's uninhibited praise in *The Lonely Life*. Writing of *Dark Victory*—"my favorite and the public's favorite part I have ever played"—she calls Edmund Goulding "one of the few all-time great directors of Hollywood."

I first met Eddie Goulding at lunch at seventeen, separated by just two years from the Kansas prairie. As an English gentleman he must have found me a startling little barbarian. He had seen me in the 1924 edition of *George White's Scandals* and wanted to make a screen test of me at the Paramount studio. When I said "No," after staring at me in a peculiar fashion, he went on, "Well then, how would you like to spend the afternoon with me?" To that I said "Yes," because I was not such a dunce as to dismiss the most joyful being I would ever meet.

We drove first to a house in the west Sixties where he left me in the cab for a half hour while he visited the "girls." Next we drove to the Hotel des Artistes to see Mrs. Novello, Ivor Novello's mother, who had become a singing coach in New York. After she and Eddie sang duets for an hour we then drove to his apartment where he was expecting Mae Murray for tea. Having written several films for her, he knew exactly how to set the scene. "She will sit here," he said, moving a small table close to a grey velour chair. "And Mae is pure—pure and eternally young." On the table he set a silver vase holding a single white rosebud. Then with a wicked smile, beside it he placed a book of pornographic drawings. "And she is regal," he warned me as she rang his doorbell. "You must curtsy when you are introduced." Mae Murray came in looking exquisitely pure and young, wearing white organdy with a pale blue sash and tiny matching blue pumps. Unfortunately, after I curtsied and she nodded regally, I had to leave for a theater rehearsal, so I never knew how she felt about the dirty pictures.

I last saw Eddie in Beverly Hills in 1938 when he was forty-seven. He had become a master of direction with *Grand Hotel,* which won the 1932 Academy production award. (Ludicrously, the direction Oscar was presented to Frank Borzage for *Bad Girl.*) Yet he remained most like an ebullient, slightly mad social director on a cruise ship. He had not withdrawn into the clouds of godly genius along with other successful directors, some of whose skeletons still rattle on lecture platforms and TV screens.

Eddie had invited me to lunch at a charming house rented for our host, Fulke, the handsome young Earl of Warwick who had come to Hollywood to heal the wounds inflicted by a recent divorce. The other guest was Jinx Falkenberg, who moved in an atmosphere of exalted "class." Hollywood producers worshipped "class" and for a time believed that this pretty, big, healthy girl was a potential star. That morning Eddie had seen a test of Jinx which he had directed at Warner Brothers. At the luncheon table she asked how it was. "Terrible," he said, suddenly coldly professional. Then in response to her expression of outrage he added, "But your behind in that nightgown was delectable—like two grapefruits tied up in a napkin." She did not join in our laughter but predictably, since I was an unprofitable woman, gave me a look of hatred and got up and left the table.

In writing the history of a life I believe absolutely that the reader cannot understand the character and deeds of the subject unless he is given a basic understanding of that person's sexual loves and hates and conflicts. It is the only way the reader can make sense out of innumerable apparently senseless actions. To paraphrase Proust: how often do we change the whole course of our lives in pursuit of a love that we will have forgotten within a few months. We flatter ourselves when we assume that we have restored the sexual integrity which was expurgated by the Victorians. It is true that many exposés are written to shock, to excite, to make money. But in serious books characters remain as baffling, as unknowable as ever. Garson Kanin's *Tracy and Hepburn* portrays the dynamic Katharine Hepburn as a sexual grotesque with "beaus." In Brooke Hayward's *Haywire,* mother and Margaret Sullavan never meet. Unwilling to deal with the sexual relationship between her mother and father, unwilling to face her mother's passionate, jealous nature, she retreats to the actress's scrapbooks as some explanation for her tragic life. Even her mother's suicide on New Year's Day in 1960 is not connected with her father, Leland Hayward's fifth marriage.

Margaret Sullavan was a certified Virginia belle, a femme fatale by conviction who had divorced Henry Fonda and William Wyler before, at the age of twenty-five, she married Leland in 1936. After he left her to marry Nancy (Slim) Hawks in 1947, this terrifyingly self-willed woman shredded her career through the following twelve years with her struggle to repossess him. When Nancy divorced him there was a flaming period of hope in 1959. Then came the news of Leland's decision to marry Pamela Churchill—and she sank into despair and death.

I too am unwilling to write the sexual truth that would make my life worth reading. I cannot unbuckle the Bible Belt. That is why I will never write my memoirs.

A Witness Speaks

THIS ALL BEGAN IN 1929. Since October, 1927, I had been a writer for the *Film-Kurier* of Berlin, a daily paper dealing with movies and theatre. In order to understand more about the techniques and styles of movies, I made a ritual of visiting the studios, to see how things were being done in this new art form of the century. (It is unfortunate that today's movie critics have given up the custom.)

One morning, I went to watch G. W. Pabst making *Diary of a Lost Girl* in a studio on the outskirts of Berlin. I arrived at a moment when they were adjusting the lights, and, with evident pride, Pabst introduced me to the actress playing the heroine of his film, a young American woman of fascinating beauty who was sitting there reading. Incredibly, what this beautiful young woman was reading was a translation of Schopenhauer's *Essays*. Of course, I assumed that this was a publicity stunt of Pabst's; he knew perfectly well that I was a university graduate. However, I grew increasingly aware of an almost magical power emanating from this strange young woman, who spoke very little, even though I addressed myself to her in English. It was Louise Brooks. I stayed on, to watch Pabst work. And this Louise Brooks, whom I scarcely heard speak, fascinated me constantly through a curious mixture of passivity and *presence* which she projected throughout the shooting.

These impressions came back to me, perfectly confirmed, when I finally saw the film. And when, much later, in 1952, I was preparing my *L'Écran Démoniaque*, I recalled this visit to Pabst's studio as I noted, apropos of two of his films, "Louise Brooks exists with an overwhelming insistence; she makes her way through these two films always enigmatically impassive. (Is she a great artist or only a dazzling creature whose beauty traps the viewer into attributing complexities to her of which she is unaware?)" The answer to this question came to me soon afterward. In the fifties, the Cinémathèque Française invited Louise Brooks to Paris, and I had the opportunity of interviewing her over an entire month. At that time—and this was characteristic of her savagely nonconformist manner—she no longer wore the bangs that had become so famous during the twenties. Quite the contrary: she systematically skimmed her hair back, off her still pure forehead. (She had kept her extraordinary profile.) One of her most ardent admirers, Ado Kyrou, was much distressed by this, not having grasped that Louise Brooks, in her uninhibited way, had compulsively turned her back on her past glamour and was living completely in the present.

I understood by then that she had walked away from films at the height of her glory, and not, like some other stars, because talking films had come along and cut short a career founded on the technique of the silents. Actually, her voice was remarkable. When I asked her why she had left films, she told me bluntly that it was because she was so bored with doing the same thing over and over. Recently, an American filmmaker visiting Germany to make a documentary for Canadian television about the surviving "figures" of Berlin in the thirties told me that, of all the personalities he had filmed, Louise Brooks was the most dazzling: that her voice was marvelous, and that he couldn't understand why American moviemakers hadn't brought her back to the screen, as they had Joan Crawford and Bette Davis.

Spending a great deal of time with Louise Brooks during her stay in Paris, I was forced to come to terms with the reality: I was in the presence of someone gifted with an astonishing personality. This presence, which had seemed so enigmatic to me during the twenties, I now saw as the creation of a lifetime, fed by her indisputable qualities of intelligence and of heart: a frankness of opinion, a lucidity in her observation of people and things, a habit of speaking her mind with total candor. I couldn't resist asking her if she had really been reading that book of Schopenhauer's I had seen in her hands. She *had* read it, and Proust as well, and many other writers one was hardly used to encountering among film people. But nothing could really astonish me any longer about this woman, whose singular strength of mind I had finally come to appreciate. Since then, we have shared a rare friendship—a sure and solid friendship, which no disagreement could destroy. And when my *Écran Démoniaque* was republished, I was able—knowing her so much better now—to write, "Today we know that Louise Brooks is not just a ravishing creature but an amazing actress gifted with an unprecedented intelligence."

Louise Brooks no longer makes films. She devotes herself to painting, in a very *direct* style, a little like that of the ancient Chinese. When I moved to a new house in 1960, she sent me one of her paintings: a tree, rendered in clean, strong lines, in shades of white, black, and gray, with a red signature done to resemble Chinese lettering. And she wrote that this present to me came from an old Chinese—"Lou Brou."

Rereading her letters is always a great pleasure, because this fiercely independent woman has, in her solitude, become an authentic writer. She has provided us with essays on the cinema of her era and on the stars she happened to encounter and to observe (Gish and Garbo, Chaplin, W. C. Fields, Humphrey Bogart)—essays striking in their evenhandedness and insight. With her customary frankness, her refusal to submit to the prejudices of the moment, she *saw* these people and events without ever going astray or deceiving herself. The publisher who planned to collect all these pieces in a book was not making a mistake; such a book would reveal the reverse side of "glamorous Hollywood." And we can rest assured that this kind of homage could not possibly go to the head of our "philosopher," who recently wrote to me on a Christmas card, not mincing words, "I shall write no more. Writing the truth for readers nourished on publicity rubbish is a useless exercise." We won't contradict her. Nevertheless, what a pity that her lifelong concern for "truth" is what is finally preventing her from giving to the world those truths it both needs and deserves.

—Lotte H. Eisner

LOUISE BROOKS (1906–1985) was one of the most influential actresses of the silent film era. She was born in Kansas and began her career at the age of fifteen as a dancer with the pioneering Denishawn company and later the Ziegfeld Follies. She starred in twenty-four films and is renowned for her iconic performances in such classics as *American Venus* and *Pandora's Box.* An outspoken critic of the Hollywood system, she was effectively black-balled and made her last movie in 1938, after which she faded into obscurity. After her retirement from Hollywood, Brooks wrote occasional essays about film that appeared in *Film Culture, Sight and Sound,* and other publications during the 1960s and 1970s, contributing to a revival of interest in her films. Some of these essays are collected in *Lulu in Hollywood.*

Filmography

STREET OF FORGOTTEN MEN

Release: Famous Players-Lasky*, 1925
Director: Herbert Brenon
Cast: Percy Marmont, Neil Hamilton

THE AMERICAN VENUS

Release: Famous Players-Lasky*, 1926
Director: Frank Tuttle
Cast: Esther Ralston, Fay Lanphier,
Lawrence Gray, Ford Sterling

A SOCIAL CELEBRITY

Release: Famous Players-Lasky*, 1926
Director: Malcolm St. Clair
Cast: Adolphe Menjou, Chester Conklin

IT'S THE OLD ARMY GAME

Release: Famous Players-Lasky*, 1926
Director: Edward Sutherland
Cast: W. C. Fields, William Gaxton, Blanche Ring

THE SHOW-OFF

Release: Famous Players-Lasky*, 1926
Director: Malcolm St. Clair
Cast: Ford Sterling, Lois Wilson, Gregory Kelly

JUST ANOTHER BLONDE

Release: First National, 1926
Director: Alfred Santell
Cast: Dorothy Mackaill, Jack Mulhall,
William Collier, Jr.

LOVE 'EM AND LEAVE 'EM

Release: Famous Players-Lasky*, 1926
Director: Frank Tuttle
Cast: Evelyn Brent, Osgood Perkins, Lawrence Gray

EVENING CLOTHES

Release: Paramount, 1927
Director: Luther Reed
Cast: Adolphe Menjou, Noah Beery, Virginia Valli,
Lilyan Tashman

ROLLED STOCKINGS

Release: Paramount, 1927
Director: Richard Rosson
Cast: James Hall, Nancy Phillips, Richard Arlen

NOW WE'RE IN THE AIR

Release: Paramount, 1927
Director: Frank Strayer
Cast: Wallace Beery, Raymond Hatton

THE CITY GONE WILD

Release: Paramount, 1927
Director: James Cruze
Cast: Thomas Meighan

A GIRL IN EVERY PORT

Release: Fox, 1928
Director: Howard Hawks
Cast: Victor McLaglen, Robert Armstrong

* Paramount release filmed in Paramount's Astoria, New York, studio.

BEGGARS OF LIFE

Release: Paramount, 1928
Director: William Wellman
Cast: Wallace Beery, Richard Arlen, Edgar Washington

THE CANARY MURDER CASE

Release: Paramount, 1929
Director: Malcolm St. Clair
Cast: William Powell, Jean Arthur

DIE BUCHSE DER PANDORA
(PANDORA'S BOX)

Release: Nero Film, Berlin, 1929
Director: G. W. Pabst
Cast: Gustav Diessl, Fritz Kortner, Franz Lederer,
Carl Goetz, Alice Roberts

DAS TAGEBUCH EINER VERLORENEN
(DIARY OF A LOST GIRL)

Release: Hom-Film, Berlin, 1929
Director: G. W. Pabst
Cast: Joseph Rovensky, Fritz Rasp, André Roanne,
Edith Meinhard, Valeska Gert, Andrews Engelmann

PRIX DE BEAUTÉ

Release: Sofar Film, Paris, 1930
Director: Augusto Genina
Cast: Georges Charlia, Jean Bradin

WINDY REILLY IN HOLLYWOOD

Release: Educational, 1931
Director: William Goodrich (Roscoe Arbuckle)
Cast: Jack Shutta, William Davidson,
Wilbur Mack, Dell Henderson, Walter Merrill

GOD'S GIFT TO WOMEN

Release: Warner Bros., 1931
Director: Michael Curtiz
Cast: Frank Fay, Laura LaPlante, Joan Blondell

IT PAYS TO ADVERTISE

Release: Paramount, 1931
Director: Frank Tuttle
Cast: Norman Foster, Carole Lombard

EMPTY SADDLES

Release: Universal, 1936
Director: Lesley Selander
Cast: Buck Jones

KING OF GAMBLERS

Release: Paramount, 1937
Director: Robert Florey
Cast: Claire Trevor, Lloyd Nolan

WHEN YOU'RE IN LOVE

Release: Columbia, 1937
Director: Robert Riskin
Cast: Grace Moore, Cary Grant

OVERLAND STAGE RAIDERS

Release: Republic, 1938
Director: George Sherman
Cast: John Wayne